RAND NATIONAL DEFENSE RESEARCH INSTITUTE

T0302825

A Persistent Threat

The Evolution of al Qa'ida and Other Salafi Jihadists

Seth G. Jones

Prepared for the Office of the Secretary of Defense

The research described in this report was prepared for the Office of the Secretary of Defense (OSD). The research was conducted within the RAND National Defense Research Institute, a federally funded research and development center sponsored by OSD, the Joint Staff, the Unified Combatant Commands, the Navy, the Marine Corps, the defense agencies, and the defense Intelligence Community.

Library of Congress Cataloging-in-Publication Data is available for this publication.

ISBN: 978-0-8330-8572-6

The RAND Corporation is a nonprofit institution that helps improve policy and decisionmaking through research and analysis. RAND's publications do not necessarily reflect the opinions of its research clients and sponsors.

Support RAND—make a tax-deductible charitable contribution at www.rand.org/giving/contribute.html

Cover image: Oleg Zabielin/Fotolia

RAND OFFICES

SANTA MONICA, CA • WASHINGTON, DC

PITTSBURGH, PA • NEW ORLEANS, LA • JACKSON, MS • BOSTON, MA

CAMBRIDGE, UK • BRUSSELS, BE

www.rand.org

Preface

This research examines the evolution of al Qa'ida and other Salafi-jihadist groups, as well as implications for U.S. policy. It was conducted within the International Security and Defense Policy Center of the RAND National Defense Research Institute, a federally funded research and development center sponsored by the Office of the Secretary of Defense, the Joint Staff, the Unified Combatant Commands, the Navy, the Marine Corps, the defense agencies, and the defense Intelligence Community.

This work may be of interest to government officials involved in counterterrorism; academics and scholars engaged in research on terrorism and counterterrorism; graduate and undergraduate students of international politics; and those in the general public interested in al Qa'ida and contemporary terrorist threats.

For more information on the RAND International Security and Defense Policy Center, see http://www.rand.org/nsrd/ndri/centers/isdp.html or contact the director (contact information is provided on the web page).

Contents

Figures and Tables

Figures

Tables

Summary

This report examines the status and evolution of al Qa'ida and other Salafi-jihadist groups, a subject of intense debate in the West. Some argue that al Qa'ida—especially core al Qa'ida—has been severely weakened, and there is no longer a major threat to the United States from Salafi-jihadist and other terrorist groups.[1] Former CIA officer Marc Sageman concluded that "al Qaeda is no longer seen as an existential threat to the West" and "the hysteria over a global conspiracy against the West has faded."[2] According to University of Chicago professor John Mearsheimer, "Terrorism—most of it arising from domestic groups—was a much bigger problem in the United States during the 1970s than it has been since the Twin Towers were toppled."[3] Brian Jenkins argued that few of America's jihadists were dedicated or competent terrorists, resembling "stray dogs" rather than "lone wolves." According to Jenkins, of the 32 jihadist terrorist plots uncovered since September 11, 2001, most never moved beyond the discussion stage. Only ten had what could be described as an operational plan, and of these, six were FBI stings. By comparison, the United States saw an average of 50 to 60 terrorist bombings a year in the 1970s and a greater number of fatalities.[4]

Some contend that the most acute threat to the United States comes from homegrown terrorists.[5] Still others maintain that al Qa'ida is resilient and remains a serious threat to the United States.[6] Finally, some claim that while the al Qa'ida organization established by Osama bin Laden is in decline, "al Qa'idism"—a decentralized amalgam of freelance extremist groups—is far from dead.[7]

Which of these views is most accurate? To better gauge the state of al Qa'ida and other Salafi-jihadist groups, this report uses a combination of qualitative and quantitative data. It examines thousands of unclassified and declassified primary source documents, such as the public statements and internal memoranda of al Qa'ida and other Salafi-jihadist leaders. In addition, it builds a database that includes information like the number of Salafi-jihadist groups, their approximate size, and their activities (attacks, fatalities, and casualties). Some of this information—particularly the database—is new and provides an important gauge of Salafi jihadists.

The report makes several arguments. First, and most important, the United States faces a serious and growing Salafi-jihadist challenge overseas. Beginning in 2010, there was a rise in the number of Salafi-jihadist groups and fighters, particularly in Syria and North Africa. There was also an increase in the number of attacks perpetrated by al Qa'ida and its affiliates. Several data points illustrate these trends:

- There was a 58-percent increase in the number of Salafi-jihadist groups from 2010 to 2013. Libya represents the most active sanctuary for Salafi-jihadist groups in North Africa, and Syria the most significant safe haven for groups in the Levant.
- The number of Salafi jihadists more than doubled from 2010 to 2013, according to both our low and high estimates. The war in Syria was the single most important attraction for Salafi-jihadist fighters.
- There was a significant increase in attacks by al Qa'ida–affiliated groups between 2007 and 2013, with most of the violence in 2013 perpetrated by the Islamic State of Iraq and al-Sham (43 percent), which eventually left al Qa'ida; al Shabaab (25 percent); Jabhat al-Nusrah (21 percent); and al Qa'ida in the Arabian Peninsula (10 percent).
- Approximately 99 percent of the attacks by al Qa'ida and its affiliates in 2013 were against "near enemy" targets in North Africa, the Middle East, and other regions outside of the West, the highest percentage of attacks against the near enemy in our database. This suggests that al Qa'ida and its affiliates have deliberately chosen to focus on the near enemy for the moment, found it increasingly difficult to strike "far enemy" targets in the West, or a combination of both.

One country in the Middle East where Salafi-jihadist groups have lost ground is Egypt, where the regime has targeted the Muhammad Jamal Network and groups in the Sinai. But the broad trends indicate that the United States needs to remain focused on countering the proliferation of Salafi-jihadist groups, which have started to resurge in North Africa and the Middle East, despite the temptations to shift attention and resources to the Asia-Pacific region and to significantly decrease counterterrorism budgets in an era of fiscal constraint.

Second, the broader Salafi-jihadist movement has become more decentralized among four tiers: core al Qa'ida in Pakistan, led by Ayman al-Zawahiri; formal affiliates that have sworn allegiance to core al Qa'ida, located in Syria, Somalia, Yemen, and North Africa; a panoply of Salafi-jihadist groups that have not sworn allegiance to al Qa'ida but are committed to establishing an extremist Islamic emirate; and inspired individuals and networks. Using the state of core al Qa'ida in Pakistan as a gauge of the movement's strengths (or weaknesses) is increasingly anachronistic for such a heterogeneous mixture of groups. In addition, while there are some similarities among Salafi jihadists, there are also substantial differences. Salafi-jihadist leaders and groups often disagree about how much, if at all, to target Western countries and their citizens; the size and global nature of their desired emirate; and their willingness to attack Shi'a. This decentralized structure creates substantial vulnerabilities for al Qa'ida and other Salafi-jihadist groups, as outlined in more detail later in the report.

Third, the threat posed by this diverse set of groups varies widely, though several of these groups pose a substantial threat to the U.S. homeland or U.S. interests overseas. Some are locally focused and have shown little interest in attacking Western targets. Others, like al Qa'ida in the Arabian Peninsula, present an immediate threat to the U.S. homeland, along with inspired individuals like the Tsarnaev brothers—the perpetrators of the April 2013 Boston Marathon bombings. In addition, some Salafi-jihadist groups pose a medium-level threat because of their desire and ability to target U.S. citizens and facilities overseas, including U.S. embassies. Examples include Ansar al-Sharia Tunisia, al Shabaab, al Qa'ida in the Islamic Maghreb, and the various Ansar al-Sharia groups in Libya.

Fourth, in response to these threats the United States should establish a more adaptive counterterrorism strategy. It should pursue long-term *engagement* in countries where there is a high threat to the United States and low local government capacity. Engagement involves the use of special operations, intelligence, diplomacy, and other capabilities to conduct precision targeting of groups and their financial, logistical, and political support networks. It often includes training, advising, and assisting local governments in their struggle against terrorism. Engagement can also involve pursuing clandestine operations against adversarial regimes that support terrorist groups. The United States should pursue *forward partnering* in countries where there is a threat to the United States but limited local government capacity. Forward partnering involves training, equipping, and advising local governments but refraining from becoming directly involved in operations. Finally, the United States should pursue *offshore balancing* in countries where there is a low threat to the United States and sufficient local government capacity or an ally (like a NATO country) willing to counter Salafi-jihadist groups. Offshore balancing involves relying on allies and local governments to counter terrorist groups while avoiding the deployment of any U.S. forces for training or other purposes. It generally includes utilizing offshore air, naval, and rapidly deployable ground forces rather than onshore combat power.

This framework and the analysis in this report highlight the need for a long-term engagement strategy—including direct U.S. involvement—in Pakistan, Afghanistan, Yemen, and possibly Syria, where there are significant terrorism threats to the United States and limited government capacity. It also highlights the importance of developing a long-term forward partnering relationship with a small set of countries in Africa (Nigeria, Algeria, Somalia, Libya, and Egypt) and the Middle East (Lebanon and Iraq), with the involvement of regional allies like Israel and Jordan. Finally, this framework identifies a subset of countries—such as Morocco and Mali—where the United States may want to encourage others (like NATO allies) to work with local governments, since the terrorist threat to the United States is limited. The United States will need to reassess these categorizations when there are changes in the threat environment and the capacity and willingness of local governments to counter terrorist groups.

In addition, this framework highlights several U.S. foreign policy issues. A complete withdrawal of U.S. military forces from Afghanistan by 2016 could seriously jeopardize U.S. security interests because of the continuing presence of Salafi-jihadist and other terrorist groups in Afghanistan and Pakistan. A growing civil war or successful Taliban-led insurgency would likely allow al Qa'ida and other terrorist groups—such as the Tehreek-e-Taliban Pakistan, Haqqani network, and Lashkar-e-Taiba—to increase their presence in Afghanistan. Al Qa'ida and associated movements would likely view an American exit from Afghanistan—if it were to happen—as their most important victory since the departure of Soviet forces from Afghanistan in 1989.

The United States should also consider a more aggressive strategy to target Salafi-jihadist groups in Syria, either clandestinely or with regional and local allies. According to our data, Salafi jihadists in Syria made up more than half the total number of Salafi jihadists worldwide in 2013 and were engaged in a growing number of attacks. In addition, Jabhat al-Nusrah and the Islamic State of Iraq and al-Sham orchestrated approximately two-thirds of al Qa'ida's attacks in 2013. U.S. counterterror operations in Syria are complicated because the Assad government is an enemy, not an ally. Nevertheless, U.S. intelligence and special operations units have several options, which are not mutually exclusive: clandestinely target Salafi-jihadist groups operating in Syria; work through allies such as Jordan, Turkey, or Saudi Arabia; and work through surrogate partners, such as Syrian rebel groups that oppose Salafi-jihadist groups in Syria.

The failure to weaken Salafi-jihadist groups in Syria will likely have serious repercussions for the United States, in part because of Syria's proximity to allies like Jordan, Turkey, Israel, and European Union countries. The access of Syrian groups such as Jabhat al-Nusrah to foreign fighters, terrorist networks in Europe, and bomb-making expertise suggest that they may already have the capability to plan, support, and potentially conduct attacks against the West.

Acknowledgments

This report would not have been possible without the help of numerous individuals. I owe an extraordinary debt of gratitude to Nathan Chandler. He collected and analyzed a substantial amount of quantitative and qualitative data, combed through hundreds of reports by al Qa'ida and other Salafi-jihadist leaders, and provided helpful comments throughout the research, writing, and editing stages. His attention to detail and analytical skills were instrumental at all stages of the report. Bruce Hoffman, Daniel Byman, Andy Liepman, and Brian Jenkins read various drafts of the report and provided candid and insightful comments, which greatly improved the substance and organization of the report. They corrected numerous errors, encouraged me to insert additional material in several places, and helped clarify several passages. Eric Peltz provided a range of useful comments, which improved the quality of the report. I would also like thank several others who helped shape my thoughts during the research and writing phase, including Mary Habeck at Johns Hopkins University, Bruce Riedel at the Brookings Institution, Thomas Joscelyn at the Foundation for Defense of Democracies, and William McCants at the Brookings Institution.

Numerous individuals in the U.S. Department of Defense, State Department, and Intelligence Community agreed to discuss al Qa'ida and Salafi-jihadist groups in the midst of busy schedules. I also spoke to government officials from several European countries, including on trips to NATO, the European Union, and Afghanistan. Thanks to all of you.

At RAND, I would like to thank Hosay Yaqub and Joy Merck for helping move the document through the writing, formatting, review, and publication process, and for their great work every day. The RAND Publications team was outstanding. Steve Kistler and Matt Byrd were a pleasure to work with, and Bryce Schoenborn did a phenomenal job editing the document, clarifying numerous passages, and shepherding it to final publication.

CHAPTER ONE

Introduction

Since al Qa'ida's establishment in 1988, the movement has experienced a series of successes and failures. These ebbs and flows can be characterized as "waves" (surges in terrorist activity) and "reverse waves" (setbacks), which varied in their duration and levels of violence.[1] The first wave picked up momentum in the 1990s and crested with the September 11, 2001, attacks. It was followed by a reversal as al Qa'ida leaders and operatives were captured or killed in Afghanistan, Pakistan, the United States, and other countries across the globe. A second wave began around 2003 after the U.S. invasion of Iraq, and was characterized by large-scale attacks across Iraq and in Casablanca, Madrid, London, and other countries. But it was followed by a reverse wave around 2006, as al Qa'ida in Iraq was severely weakened, British and American intelligence agencies foiled several plots, and U.S. drone strikes killed senior al Qa'ida operatives in Pakistan. A third wave surged between 2007 and 2009 following the rise of al Qa'ida in the Arabian Peninsula, and was followed by a reverse wave with the death of Osama bin Laden in 2011 and other senior leaders. Today, there is considerable disagreement about the strength and composition of al Qa'ida and the broader milieu of Salafi-jihadist groups.

To assess the state of al Qa'ida and Salafi-jihadist groups, this report asks three sets of questions. First, how should the movement be characterized today? How is it organized, what are the objectives of Salafi-jihadist groups, and what is their strategy (or strategies)? Second, how strong (or weak) is the movement today? Third, what strategies should the United States pursue to weaken al Qa'ida and the broader milieu of Salafi-jihadist groups?

Key Definitions

This report focuses on a particular strand of militant Sunni Islamism: Salafi-jihadist groups. As explained in more detail in the next chapter, a group is defined as Salafi-jihadist based on two criteria. First, the group emphasizes the importance of returning to a "pure" Islam, that of the Salaf, the pious ancestors. Second, the group believes that violent jihad is *fard 'ayn* (a personal religious duty).[2] *Fard 'ayn* includes tasks every Muslim is required to perform, such as *zakat* (almsgiving), *hajj* (the pilgrimage to Mecca), *salat* (daily prayers), *sawm* (fasting during Ramada), and the *shahada* (accepting Muhammad as God's messenger).[3] Jihad is not one of these five pillars. It is, instead, a collective duty (*fard kifaya*) under certain circumstances. A *fard kifaya* is an act that is obligatory for the Muslim community collectively. But if it is sufficiently carried out by some members of the Muslim community, then other Muslims do not have to perform it. An example is the prayer performed at a Muslim burial. Still, most Salafi jihadists consider violent jihad an individual duty, or *fard 'ayn*.[4] Ayman al-Zawahiri, among others, emphasized both Salafism and armed jihad.[5]

This report focuses on Salafi-jihadist groups for several reasons. First, they represent a threat to the United States and its allies, since most Salafi-jihadist groups consider America an enemy. As explained later in the report, however, some Salafi-jihadist groups have plotted attacks against the U.S. homeland and U.S. interests overseas, while others are focused on local enemies. Second, many Salafi-jihadist groups are willing to kill civilians in ways that terrorist groups have historically eschewed. Brian Jenkins wrote in the 1970s that "terrorists want a lot of people watching, not a lot of people dead," a statement he later amended with the rise of organizations like al Qa'ida that wanted a lot of people watching *and* a lot of people dead.[6] Salafi jihadists are willing to kill large numbers of civilians they consider apostates, including Muslims, making the potential for wanton destruction particularly acute. Third, al Qa'ida is Salafi-jihadist. To be clear, most Salafi-jihadist groups are not al Qa'ida. That is, they have not sworn *bay'at* to al Qa'ida leaders, and al Qa'ida has not incorporated them into the movement as formal affiliates. Nevertheless, many have been willing to cooperate with al Qa'ida or its affiliates when it suits them.

Consequently, this analysis does not examine all Islamist groups (those organizations attempting to build an Islamic state).[7] It does not analyze, for example, the Muslim Brotherhood, which is a pan-Islamic social movement established by the Islamic scholar and schoolteacher Hassan al-Banna. It also does not analyze in detail the Taliban and other extreme Deobandi groups in South Asia, which are committed to establishing an Islamic emirate. Nor does it focus on militant Shi'a groups, such as Hezbollah. Some of these groups pose a threat to the United States, its interests abroad, and allies, though the religious views of these terrorist groups are different from—and often at odds with—Salafi jihadists. Still, the U.S. strategic options outlined at the end of this report are broadly applicable to a wide range of terrorist and insurgent groups, not just Salafi jihadists.

In addition, when discussing al Qa'ida, this report refers to the central leadership in Pakistan and the affiliated groups whose leaders have sworn *bay'at*, or loyalty, to core al Qa'ida, which supports the relationship.[8] These groups include al Qa'ida in the Islamic Maghreb (AQIM), al Qa'ida in the Arabian Peninsula (AQAP) based in Yemen, al Shabaab based in Somalia, and Jabhat al-Nusrah based in Syria. The Islamic State of Iraq and al-Sham (ISIS) was also an al Qa'ida affiliate until early 2014, when it was expelled by core al Qa'ida leaders. While al Qa'ida has become more decentralized over time, its leadership cadre in Pakistan still maintains a formal relationship with a small number of affiliates.[9] Unfortunately, numerous journalists and pundits have erroneously used the term "al Qa'ida" to refer to a wide range of groups, including many whose leaders have never sworn allegiance to the organization.

Research Design

This study utilized both qualitative and quantitative data. First, it compiled and analyzed thousands of documents, including the writings, statements, and internal memorandums of al Qa'ida and other Salafi-jihadist leaders. The goal is to better understand their objectives and strategies. As political scientists Alexander George and Timothy McKeown argue, it is important to understand "what stimuli the actors attend to; the decision process that makes use of these stimuli to arrive at decisions; the actual behavior that then occurs; the effect of various institutional arrangements on attention, processing, and behavior; and the effect of other variables of interest on attention, processing, and behavior."[10] Consequently, the study reviewed the primary source works of al Qa'ida's core leaders in Pakistan (led by Ayman al-Zawahiri) and al Qa'ida affiliates in Iraq (led by Abu Bakr al-Baghdadi, or 'Abu Du'a) through their 2014 break-up with al Qa'ida, North Africa (led by Abdelmalek Droukdal), Syria (led by Abu Muhammad al-Jawlani), Somalia (led by Ahmed Abdi aw-Mohammed), and Yemen (led by Nasir al-Wuhayshi). It also analyzed the writings and statements of other Salafi-jihadist leaders. Among other sources, it examined a range of documents from such sources as the Harmony Database at the Combating Terrorism Center at West Point, as well as al Qa'ida documents found by organizations such as the Associated Press.

Second, the study compiled and analyzed data on the number and geographic location of Salafi-jihadist groups; number of Salafi jihadists; and number and type of attacks, fatalities, and casualties by some Salafi-jihadist groups. There are, of course, methodological challenges in any study of al Qa'ida and other Salafi-jihadist groups, as there are of terrorist groups more broadly. There are, for instance, knowledge gaps in understanding the daily operations of clandestine networks trying to survive in the face of government surveillance efforts and assassinations. Since the life expectancy of jihadist websites can be short because of government actions, it is difficult to provide the reader with a way to check all quotations. But experience shows that most important texts are circulating on a number of websites and could be retrieved even if the given site has disappeared or its URL has changed. Another challenge is transcription. I have decided not to adopt a uniform transcription across all proper names in the footnotes because it will make the checking of sources almost impossible. When I quote a name from a website or transcription service, or use it in a citation, I generally use the transcriptions of the sites to allow the reader to check. Apart from the quotations and citations, however, I have tried to use an identical transcription throughout the report.[11]

In addition, there is often wide variation in the names and spelling of individuals and groups. Take, as an example, the former al Qa'ida affiliate in Iraq. It is referred to in the media and by policymakers as al Qa'ida in Iraq (AQI), the Islamic State of Iraq and Syria (ISIS), the Islamic State of Iraq and al-Sham (ISIS), and the Islamic State of Iraq and the Levant (ISIL). All refer to the same group. I have chosen to utilize the Islamic State of Iraq and al-Sham, in part since that is how group members often refer to themselves.

Outline of the Report

The rest of this report is divided into several chapters. Chapter Two examines al Qa'ida and the broader movement of Salafi-jihadist groups today by assessing their organizational structure, objectives, and strategies. It also analyzes why the movement has become more decentralized over time. Chapter Three focuses on the capabilities of al Qa'ida and other Salafi-jihadist groups and examines trends in the number of groups, levels of violence, and other factors. It also explores why there has been an expansion in the number of Salafi-jihadist groups over time. Chapter Four outlines strategic options for the United States and implications for U.S. counterterrorism policy in such countries as Syria and Afghanistan.

CHAPTER TWO

A Decentralized Movement

In May 2013, al Qa'ida leader Ayman al-Zawahiri sent a terse note to Abu Bakr Al-Baghdadi (also known as 'Abu Du'a), the emir of the Islamic State of Iraq and al-Sham, and Abu Muhammad al-Jawlani, the emir of Jabhat al-Nusrah. Zawahiri's purpose was straightforward: to resolve an escalating dispute between the two leaders over command-and-control arrangements. Jawlani wanted his organization to become a separate al Qa'ida affiliate that reported directly to core al Qa'ida in Pakistan. Baghdadi wanted Jabhat al-Nusrah to continue under his umbrella. The roots of the conflict dated back to 2011. As the insurgency in Syria began, Baghdadi had sent Jawlani and other operatives to Syria in 2011 to help overthrow the Syrian regime. As Jawlani recalled, Baghdadi "approved our plan to support the oppressed in al-Sham [Syria], and gave us money . . . and sent us a few brethren."[1] Over time, Jawlani's organization, Jabhat al-Nusrah, became increasingly powerful and self-sufficient, securing its own donors and funding from sources in the Persian Gulf and Levant, developing sophisticated bomb-making capabilities, and attracting a growing number of fighters.

Threatened by Jabhat al-Nusrah's growing power, Baghdadi attempted to rein in the organization. In April 2013, Baghdadi publicly announced: "It's now time to declare in front of the people of the Levant and world that Jabhat al-Nusrah is but an extension of the Islamic State of Iraq and part of it." He continued by clarifying what that meant: "So we declare while relying on Allah: The cancellation of the name 'Islamic State of Iraq,' and the cancellation of the name, 'Jabhat al-

Nusrah,' and gathering them under one name, the 'Islamic State in Iraq and al-Sham.'"[2] Jawlani objected. Baghdadi had not informed him of the announcement and, besides, he strongly opposed coming under the command and control of the Islamic State of Iraq and al-Sham. In an angry retort, he shot back, "The reality is that we were not consulted or informed about this alleged speech."[3] He then went further, pledging *bay'at* (allegiance) to al Qa'ida leader Ayman al-Zawahiri. The act was a deliberate effort by Jawlani to demonstrate to his own followers, al Qa'ida leaders in Pakistan, and Baghdadi that Jabhat al-Nusrah's command and control went directly to core al Qa'ida in Pakistan. It was a blatant rebuke to Baghdadi. Over the next month, tensions escalated between Jabhat al-Nusrah and Islamic State of Iraq and al-Sham leaders, forcing Zawahiri to step in.

In a carefully worded letter, Zawahiri thanked both for their steadfast work for al Qa'ida, though he expressed dismay that "regrettably, we have heard the news [of the dispute] from the media."[4] He then explained that he had patiently listened to both sides, consulted with al Qa'ida leaders in Pakistan, and come to a decision. Zawahiri adjudicated in favor of Jawlani, announcing Jabhat al-Nusrah as "an independent entity for [al Qa'ida], under the general command."[5] Zawahiri then appointed Abu Khalid al-Suri, who was later killed, to serve as a mediator between the two sides.[6] In a brazen announcement, Baghdadi rejected Zawahiri's decision, arguing that he had "several shariah and method-based issues" with the ruling. He promised that "the Islamic State in Iraq and al-Sham remains as long as we have a pulse or an eye that blinks."[7] In January 2014, Zawahiri again urged the two al Qa'ida affiliates in Syria to end factional fighting, but with little success.[8] When his mediation efforts failed in February 2014, Zawahiri dismissed the Islamic State of Iraq and al-Sham from al Qa'ida.[9]

This three-way debate between al Qa'ida leaders in Pakistan, Syria, and Iraq highlighted a number of issues. It showed the evolving geographic scope of al Qa'ida, especially its spread to Syria beginning in 2011. It also illustrated core al Qa'ida's difficulties in managing distant affiliates. In light of these developments, this chapter asks several questions: How are al Qa'ida and the broader Salafi-jihadist movement structured? What are their objectives? And how have their structure and objectives evolved over time?

The chapter makes several arguments. First, the Salafi-jihadist movement has become more decentralized over time and increasingly heterogeneous. It includes core al Qa'ida, formal affiliates that have sworn allegiance to al Qa'ida leaders, groups that have not sworn allegiance but are committed to the Salafi-jihadist ideology, and inspired individuals and networks. Second, while there are some similarities among Salafi jihadists, there are also substantial differences. Salafi-jihadist leaders and groups disagree about how much, if at all, to target Western countries and their citizens; the size and global nature of their desired emirate; eagerness to attack Shi'a; and other issues, such as their involvement in social services, implementation of draconian policies against local populations, and the appropriateness of targeting civilians. Third, al Qa'ida and other Salafi-jihadist groups have likely decentralized for two reasons: widespread variation in objectives, geography, ethnic groups, personalities, and other factors that make it difficult to coordinate; and counterterrorism pressure that has forced them underground and complicated communication across the movement. This decentralized structure makes al Qa'ida and other Salafi-jihadist groups vulnerable to exploitation.

A Diffuse Structure

Over the first decade and a half of al Qa'ida's existence, Osama bin Laden oversaw a somewhat hierarchical organizational structure.[10] As al Qa'ida's internal documents show, it had employment contracts that specified vacation policies, roles and responsibilities for different jobs, security memos written by a specialized security committee, and standardized questionnaires for those arriving at training camps.[11] Al Qa'ida was composed of a shura council and several committees, such as those dedicated to military, media, finance, and religious issues. The shura council was the most powerful committee, and served as an advisory body to Osama bin Laden, who was its emir.[12] Despite this centralized apparatus, al Qa'ida and the broader movement inspired by

Osama bin Laden included a degree of decentralization. The February 1998 fatwa signed by Osama bin Laden and others, for instance, included a number of organizations, such as the Jihad Group in Egypt and Jamiat-ul-Ulema-e-Pakistan, that pledged to "kill the Americans and their allies . . . in any country in which it is possible to do it."[13] But following the overthrow of the Taliban regime and al Qa'ida's loss of sanctuary in Afghanistan, the movement began to decentralize.[14]

Today, it can be divided into four tiers: core al Qa'ida, affiliated al Qa'ida groups, other Salafi-jihadiast groups, and inspired individuals and networks.[15]

Core al Qa'ida includes the organization's leaders, most of whom are based in Pakistan. Al Qa'ida leaders refer to this broader area as Khurasan, a historical reference to the territory that included Persia, Central Asia, Afghanistan, and parts of northwestern Pakistan during the Umayyad and Abbasid caliphates.[16] Core al Qa'ida is led by Ayman al-Zawahiri, who is buttressed by such figures as Abdullah al-Shami. There are still a few Americans in core al Qa'ida (such as al-Shami and Adam Gadahn) and operatives that have lived in America (such as Adnan el Shukrijumah). Al Qa'ida's senior leadership retains some oversight of the affiliates and, when necessary, may attempt to adjudicate disputes among affiliates or provide strategic guidance. But Zawahiri's failure to mediate the dispute between Jabhat al-Nusrah and the Islamic State of Iraq and al-Sham highlights core al Qa'ida's limitations. Around July 2013, Zawahiri took an unprecedented step by appointing Nasir al-Wuhayshi, the emir of al Qa'ida in the Arabian Peninsula, as his deputy, elevating the importance of Yemen for core al Qa'ida.

The next tier includes affiliated groups that became formal branches of al Qa'ida. What distinguishes "affiliates" from other types of Salafi-jihadist groups is the decision by their emirs to swear *bay'at* to al Qa'ida leaders, which is then formally accepted by al Qa'ida leaders. These organizations include al Qa'ida in the Arabian Peninsula (based in Yemen), al Shabaab (based in Somalia), al Qa'ida in the Islamic Maghreb (based in Algeria and neighboring countries), and Jabhat al-Nusrah (based in Syria). All of the affiliates were established within the past decade: al Qa'ida in the Islamic Magrheb in 2006; al Qa'ida in the

Arabian Peninsula in 2009; al Shabaab in 2012; and Jabhat al-Nusrah in 2013.[17] As previously noted, core al Qa'ida formally separated itself from the Islamic State of Iraq and al-Sham in January 2014. Figure 2.1 highlights core al Qa'ida and affiliates.

Next are a series of other Salafi-jihadist groups, some of whom established a direct relationship with al Qa'ida. But they were not created by core al Qa'ida, have not become formal members, and their leaders have not sworn *bay'at* to core al Qa'ida. This arrangement allows these Salafi-jihadist groups to remain independent and pursue their own goals in general, but to work with al Qa'ida for specific operations or training purposes if their interests converge. As illustrated in the Appendix, there are a substantial number of other Salafi-jihadist groups across Africa (such as Ansar al-Sharia Libya and Harakat Ansar al-Din), Asia (such as Jemaah Islamiya and the East Turkestan Islamic Movement), the Middle East (such as Ansar Bayt al-Maqdis and Ziyad al-Jarrah Battalions), and the Caucasus (such as Imarat Kavkaz).

Figure 2.1
Core al Qa'ida and Its Affiliates

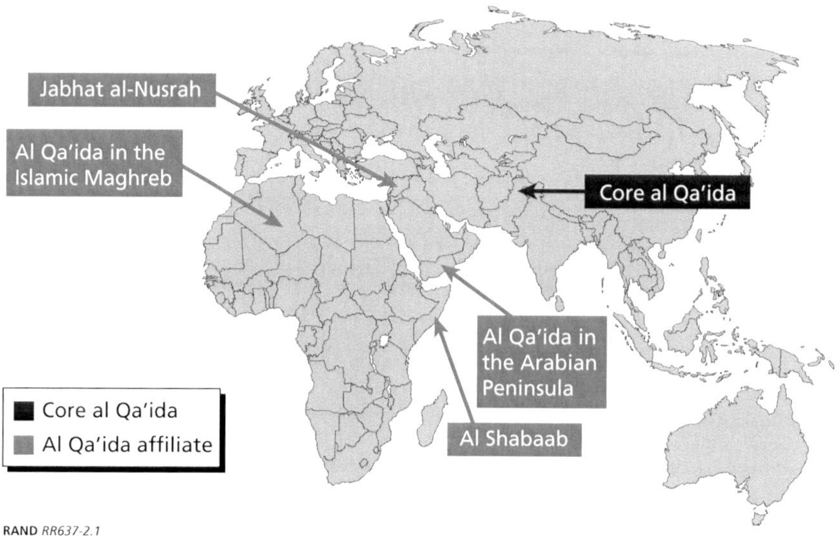

RAND *RR637-2.1*

Finally, the inspired individuals and networks include those with no direct contact to core al Qa'ida and little or no organizational structure, but who are inspired by the al Qa'ida cause and outraged by perceived oppression of Muslims in Afghanistan, Chechnya, Palestine, and other countries.[18] They tend to be motivated by a hatred of the West and regimes across the Muslim world. Without direct support, these individuals and networks tend to be amateurish.[19] But they can occasionally be lethal. On November 19, 2009, Nidal Malik Hasan walked into the Soldier Readiness Center at Fort Hood, Texas, a facility where soldiers were processed before and after deployment. He bowed his head for several seconds and then stood up and opened fire, screaming "Allahu Akbar!" Hasan methodically killed 13 people, mostly soldiers, and wounded 43 others before he was shot, disarmed, and captured.[20]

Differing Ideological Views and Objectives

Based on this increasingly decentralized structure, it is important to re-examine the ideology and objectives of Salafi-jihadist groups today. Most believe that the early generations of Muslims set the model that all succeeding generations should observe, especially in their beliefs, understanding of the core Islamic texts, methods of worship, piety, and conduct. Modern-day Islam had become corrupt, Sayyid Qutb wrote in his book *Milestones*, and he compared the modern Muslim states with *jahiliyya*.[21] As used in the Qur'an, *jahiliyya* describes the state of ignorance in which Arabs were supposed to have lived before the revelation of Islam to the Prophet Muhammad at the beginning of the seventh century.[22] Other historical figures, such as Ibn Taymiyyah, the Muslim theologian who lived in the late thirteenth and early fourteenth centuries, had long emphasized a strict adherence to the Qur'an and practices of the Prophet Muhammad.[23]

Salafi jihadists support both Salafism and violent jihad. Most Salafi jihadists view violent jihad as a *duty* for Muslims.[24] Ayman al-Zawahiri argued in 2013 that there "is no honor for us except through Jihad," emphasizing that jihad is "obligatory."[25] As Zawahiri also contended, the "first orientation is the orientation of Jihad, Ribaat [guarding the frontiers], resolve, defense of Islam's sanctuary and sanctities, and adherence to the principles of 'Aqeedah [Islamic theology]."[26] In order to establish emirates, most Salafi jihadists seek to replace regimes through an insurgency—a political-military campaign by a substate group (or groups) to secede from a country or overthrow a government.[27] The use of terrorism as a tactic rarely resulted in groups achieving their objectives; studies indicate that terrorists succeed less than 10 percent of the time.[28] But groups that resort to insurgency fare better than terrorists, winning about 30 percent of the time.[29] Captured al Qa'ida documents show that bin Laden and Zawahiri chose accordingly, emphasizing insurgency as the primary vehicle of its jihad against apostate governments.[30]

In addition, most Salafi jihadists emphasize the importance of *tawhid* (the oneness of God) and *shari'a* (Islamic law) in areas they control.[31] In two of his key works, *In the Shade of the Qur'an* and *Milestones*, Sayyid Qutb pleaded for contemporary Muslims to build a new community—an Islamic emirate based on *shari'a*—much like the Prophet Muhammad had done a thousand years earlier.[32] An emirate refers literally to a territory ruled by an "emir," which is sometimes translated as "commander," "prince," "governor," or "ruler." In early Islamic history, emirates denoted local Muslim principalities or small kingdoms nominally subordinate to the Islamic caliphate, established as part of Islam's steady expansion eastward and westward. Salafi-jihadist leaders have echoed the importance of establishing *shari'a* in areas they control.[33]

Within Islam, the Salafi-jihadist view of *shari'a* is extreme. Most believe *shari'a* should replace other forms of government, including democracy.[34] In fact, al Qa'ida leaders have been particularly critical of other Sunni groups, such as the Muslim Brotherhood in Egypt and Hamas in Palestinian territory, precisely because they have been willing to join the political process. In 2013, Zawahiri argued that the most important mistake by the Muslim Brotherhood in Egypt was its attempt to take power through democracy. "What happened is the biggest proof for the failure of taking the way of democracy," Zawahiri chided Muslim Brotherhood leaders. "In the beginning, we have to recognize that legitimacy isn't in elections and democracy, but legitimacy is the shar'ia, since who is outside the shar'ia is out of the legitimacy, and the subordinate to the rulings of the shar'ia is obedient and concordant with the legitimacy."[35] Since religious law is preeminent, Salafi jihadists argue, democracy and other political forms of government are anathema.[36]

Beyond these commonalities, however, there are numerous differences among groups, which likely increased as the number of groups and fighters expanded. Salafi-jihadist objectives can vary in several ways.

Far Enemy Versus Near Enemy

One disagreement is over how much, if at all, to attack Western countries and their citizens. For many Salafi jihadists, their primary goal is to overthrow regimes in Muslim countries.[37] The governments in these areas constitute the "near enemy," or *al-Adou al-Qareeb*.[38] They either lack the will or the capabilities to strike Western countries. But some individuals also seek to target the United States and other Western countries that represent the "far enemy," or *al-Adou al-Baeed*, and that support regimes in Africa, the Middle East, and Asia. Targeting the far enemy was critical for Osama bin Laden. As Ayman al-Zawahiri also emphasized in his "General Guidelines for Jihad," published in 2013, al Qa'ida's "military work firstly targets the head of (international) disbelief, America and its ally Israel, and secondly its local allies that rule our countries." He explained that the "purpose of targeting America is to exhaust her and bleed her to death" by, in part, baiting the United States to overreact so that it suffered substantial human and financial losses.[39]

Other groups, such as al Qa'ida in the Arabian Peninsula, also targeted far-enemy countries and their citizens in the region. As al Qa'ida in the Arabian Peninsula emir Nasir al-Wuhayshi explained, legitimate targets in near-enemy countries include Western tourists because they "are part of the Crusader campaign" and, in his view, they are primarily traveling as Christian missionaries, "callers for pornography and spreading of debauchery," or spies.[40] Resource limitations can also impact the debate between attacking far and near enemies, since far-enemy plots are likely to be more expensive and complicated than plots in their home countries.

The United States is, of course, not the only foreign target. Al Qa'ida in the Islamic Maghreb leaders like Abu Musab Abdel Madoud (also known as Abdelmalek Droukdal) have repeatedly encouraged attacks against French targets because of Paris' support to North African regimes, French military operations against Salafi-jihadist groups in countries like Mali, and religious and sociocultural practices like French bans on head scarves and veils.[41] In addition, al Shabaab leaders in Somalia have supported strikes against French and British targets, as well several governments in the region, such as Kenya. As one Shabaab document summarized: "The French and the English are to be treated equally: Their blood and their money are halal wherever they may be. No Muslim in any part of the world may cooperate with them in any way. Cooperating with the French is the same as cooperating with the English: it leads to apostasy and expulsion from Islam, regardless of the nationality and identity of the conspirer."[42] As discussed in more detail in the next chapter, though, most Salafi-jihadist groups are not actively targeting the far enemy.

Geographic Scope

There is also wide variation among Salafi jihadists about the scope of their desired emirate. Some groups, particularly the al Qa'ida leadership in Pakistan, remain committed to establishing a caliphate that extends from southern Europe to Africa, the Middle East, and parts of Asia. As Ayman al-Zawahiri acknowledged, his goal is to "liberate all occupied Muslim lands and reject each and every international treaty, agreement, and resolution which gives the infidels the right to seize Muslim lands, such as Israel's seizure of Palestine, Russia's seizure of Chechnya and the Muslim Caucasus, India's seizure of Kashmir, Spain's seizure of Ceuta and Melilla, and China's seizure of East Turkestan."[43] This view is not new. Core al Qa'ida leaders have been remarkably consistent in their desire for a pan-Islamic caliphate.[44] To be clear, however, al Qa'ida's leadership is not interested in establishing a truly *global* caliphate, but rather one that is roughly limited to the territory illustrated in Figure 2.2.[45]

Figure 2.2
Notional Map of Ayman al-Zawahiri's Envisioned Caliphate

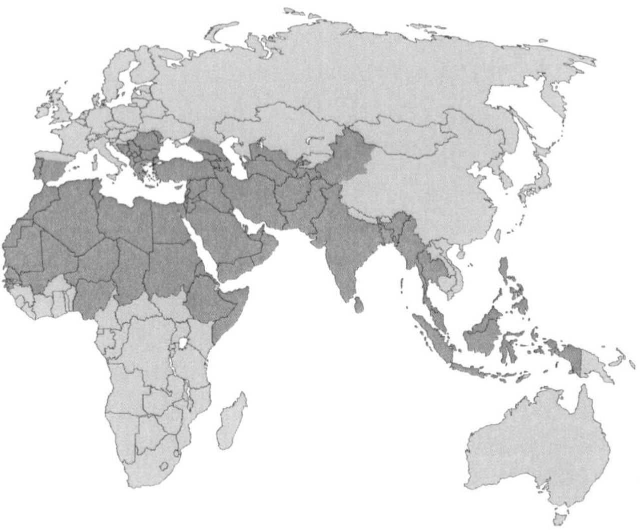

RAND *RR637-2.2*

This expansive view of a pan-Islamic caliphate is not shared by all Salafi-jihadist groups. Others are focused on establishing an emirate in specific countries or regions. Islamic State of Iraq and al-Sham leaders, for example, have primarily concentrated on controlling an area that includes Iraq and the broader Levant. Islamic State of Iraq and al-Sham emir Abu Bakr al-Baghdadi has called for "demolishing the Sykes-Picot borders" and establishing a regional emirate, a reference to the 1916 Sykes-Picot Agreement between the United Kingdom and France that divided the Arab provinces of the Ottoman Empire outside the Arabian Peninsula into areas of British and French influence.[46] Al Qa'ida in the Islamic Maghreb leaders have also focused on establishing regional emirates, including in the Sahel and Maghreb. As its emir, Abu Musab Abdel Madoud, explained, "As far as our goals concerning the Islamic Maghreb, there are plenty. But most importantly to rescue our countries from the tentacles of these criminal regimes that betrayed their religion. Because they are all secretions of the colonialism that invaded our country in the last two centuries, and enabled those regimes to govern."[47] Consequently, al Qa'ida in the Islamic Maghreb has concentrated on overthrowing governments in countries like Algeria, Mali, Tunisia, and Libya. In the Persian Gulf, al Qa'ida in the Arabian Peninsula leaders have generally focused on establishing an emirate in the Arabian Peninsula, including Yemen and Saudi Arabia.[48]

Still other Salafi-jihadist groups are interested in establishing emirates *within* specific states. Boko Haram leaders in Nigeria, for instance, have focused on establishing an emirate in Nigeria. In fact, many Salafi-jihadist groups—such as Ansar al-Sharia Libya, Harakat Ansar al-Din, and the Islamic Movement of Uzbekistan—have parochial goals of establishing emirates in their respective countries of origin.

Attacking Shi'a

There is also significant variation in the willingness of groups to attack Shi'a, who Salafi jihadists generally refer to as "Safavid Rafida." *Rafida* roughly translates as "deserters" or "defectors," and is a derogatory reference to Shi'a Muslims because they do not recognize Abu Bakr and his successors as having been legitimate rulers (*Rashidun*) of the early Muslim community. Safavid is a reference to the Safavid dynasty that ruled from 1501 to 1722, which controlled Persia and parts of South Asia, Central Asia, and the Caucasus during its peak. Among Salafi jihadists, Islamic State of Iraq and al-Sham leaders have frequently targeted Shi'a. As former al Qa'ida in Iraq leader Abu Mus'ab al-Zarqawi explained:

> [They are] the insurmountable obstacle, the lurking snake, the crafty and malicious scorpion, the spying enemy, and the penetrating venom. We here are entering a battle on two levels. One, evident and open, is with an attacking enemy and patent infidelity. [Another is] a difficult, fierce battle with a crafty enemy who wears the garb of a friend, manifests agreement, and calls for comradeship, but harbors ill will and twists up peaks and crests. Theirs is the legacy of the Batini bands that traversed the history of Islam and left scars on its face that time cannot erase. The unhurried observer and inquiring onlooker will realize that

> Shi'ism is the looming danger and the true challenge. They are the enemy. Beware of them. Fight them. By God, they lie.[49]

Abu Bakr al-Baghdadi, the Islamic State of Iraq and al-Sham's emir, denounced Shi'a as apostates and encouraged violent jihad against them: "I direct my call to all the Muslim youth and men all over the world, and call them to make Hijrah to us to consolidate the pillars of the State of Islam and perform Jihad against the Safavid Rafida—the Magian Shiites."[50] Jabhat al-Nusrah leaders also targeted Shi'a, fighting against Hezbollah in Syria and referring to Shi'a as blasphemous.[51]

But other Salafi jihadists, including some al Qa'ida leaders in Pakistan, sometimes encouraged a more cautious approach, even though they were deeply critical of Shi'a.[52] In a letter to Abu Mus'ab al-Zarqawi, for instance, Zawahiri explained that while the Shi'a were a religious school "based on excess and falsehood," targeting them would cripple al Qa'ida's support among the broader Muslim community in Iraq. "Is it something that is unavoidable?" he asked. "Or, is it something that can be put off until the force of the mujahed movement in Iraq gets stronger?"[53] Despite the actions against Shi'a among al Qa'ida leaders in Iraq and Syria, most Salafi-jihadist groups have not focused on armed jihad against Shi'a. In some cases, such as in North and East Africa, this caution may be because there are few or no Shi'a communities in their countries. In other cases, it may be because of a preference to target near- or far-enemy regimes instead. Core al Qa'ida leaders have not been involved in attacks against Shi'a in Afghanistan or Pakistan, though there are some local groups, such as Lashkar-e-Jhangvi, that have attacked Shi'a.

Other Differences

There is some variation among Salafi-jihadist groups across a miscellaneous range of issues. Some al Qa'ida in the Arabian Peninsula leaders, for example, have encouraged operatives to refrain from implementing overly draconian policies to prevent a loss of local support. As Nasir al-Wuhayshi explained to al Qa'ida in the Islamic Maghreb leaders: "But Allah has sent you to this Umma to move them toward the right path. You have to be kind to them and make room for compassion and for leniency. Try to win them over through the conveniences of life and by taking care of their daily needs like food, electricity and water." He continued: "You can't beat people for drinking alcohol when they don't even know the basics of how to pray. We have to first stop the great sins, and then move gradually to the lesser and lesser ones."[54] This explanation was a practical approach to ruling in recently controlled territory. It reflected a desire to prevent the alienation of the local population by applying a draconian interpretation of shar'ia too quickly. Indeed, groups like al Qa'ida in the Arabian Peninsula and Jabhat al-Nusrah have urged their operatives to support the education of youth, water projects, electricity generation, sewage, and food programs to win popular support.[55] These are practices that have been more historically associated with groups like Hezbollah in Lebanon. Jabhat al-Nusrah's decision to seek the support of local populations may have reflected a desire to learn from the mistakes of al Qa'ida in Iraq that contributed to the 2006 Awakening in al Anbar and other areas.[56]

In addition, there is variation about attacking non-Muslim communities living in Muslim lands. For some Salafi-jihadist groups, all non-Muslims (and even some Muslim populations like Shi'a and Sufi) are targets. But others have urged followers to refrain from targeting non-Muslim communities unless attacked by them. As Ayman al-Zawahiri explained, "Avoid meddling with Christian, Sikh, and Hindu communities living in Muslim lands. If they transgress, then a response proportionate to the transgression should suffice. This response should be accompanied with a statement that we do not seek to initiate a fight against them . . . and that we are keen to live with them in a peaceful manner after an Islamic state is established."[57]

Salafi-jihadist groups have disagreed about other issues. Al Qa'ida leader Ayman al-Zawahiri, for instance, criticized Boko Haram's indiscriminate attacks and targeting of civilians. He also chastised some groups for conducting suicide operations that unnecessarily killed civilians, hit the wrong target, or undermined local support. "Along with this expansion in martyrdom-seeking actions were deviation and transgression," Zawahari wrote in the second edition of *Winds of Paradise*, published in 2014, "which must be corrected and recognized."[58] Salafi jihadists have also disagreed over the Islamic concept of *takfir*, or disbelief. Some have condemned all Muslims who do not subscribe to their extreme interpretation of Islam as *takfiris*, potentially punishable by death. Others have taken a more lenient approach.

Causes of Decentralization

There are several possible reasons for al Qa'ida's decentralization. First, al Qa'ida and other Salafi-jihadist groups have likely decentralized to survive government crackdowns. Hierarchical groups are vulnerable to decapitation strategies, in which governments attempt to weaken or destroy the group by capturing or killing its leadership.[59] Government pressure can force cells and members into hiding, increasing the likelihood of dispersal. This can be particularly true if terrorists are forced to curb the use of cell phones, satellite phones, e-mail, and other types of electronic communications among group members because of monitoring by foreign intelligence agencies. There is some evidence that al Qa'ida decentralized for survival reasons. A 2002 meeting in Iran involving al Qa'ida leaders, for instance, was apparently a direct result of "the loss of key leaders" by U.S.-led counterterrorism raids and a recognition that al Qa'ida "could no longer exist as a hierarchy" without risking the collapse of the group.[60] After the death of Osama bin Laden and other leaders in Pakistan from drone strikes and raids, al Qa'ida leaders warned their adherents in a public communiqué that the movement's survival hinged on "taking precautions, working in total secrecy, and making use of all means to do damage to the enemy."[61]

There are numerous historical examples of terrorist and insurgent groups that decentralized because of government repression. During the Malayan Emergency that lasted from 1948 to 1957, for example, the Malayan Communist Party established an increasingly decentralized structure. Initially, the political apparatus included a Central Committee and a series of State, District, and Branch Committees—partly in the jungle and partly outside the country. The Malayan People's Anti-British Army mobilized eight regiments and later increased to ten.[62] Beginning around 1951, however, the Malayan Communist Party decentralized in response to British infiltration and counterinsurgency successes. This reorganization created serious problems for the Malayan Communist Party, whose lower-level echelons did not receive specific orders or instructions either from outside the country or from their own superior headquarters.[63] There are numerous other examples. In Sudan, the Anya Nya was fragmented for much of the war that lasted from 1963 to 1972, in part because of government repression. As one analysis concluded, the Anya Nya "did not develop into a politically organized movement under a disciplined military leadership," but rather "consisted of scattered local resistance bands."[64]

Second, the decentralization of Salafi-jihadist groups is likely caused by fragmentation from increasingly divergent objectives, geography, ethnic groups, personalities, and other factors in a heterogeneous movement. As already noted, there is considerable variation in objectives among Salafi jihadists, which makes it difficult to coordinate activities. The same is true with geography, since Salafi-jihadist groups are spread across multiple continents from Algeria along the Mediterranean Sea to Indonesia in the Indian Ocean. There are also a variety of ethnic groups, languages, and cultures that span this area, from Tuaregs in northern Mali to Yemeni tribes along the Gulf of Aden. In addition, Salafi-jihadist groups include a wide range of leaders, from the fiery Mokhtar Belmokhtar to the more philosophical Zawahiri.

This variation makes it virtually impossible to centralize and coordinate activities because of what social scientists refer to as a "principal-agent problem."[65] A principal (an insurgent or terrorist leader) needs to set in place a system of incentives and penalties so that an agent (a member of the group) will perform as the principal expects. Lower-level fighters often take actions that cannot easily be observed and evaluated by their superiors. The difficulty of monitoring dispersed operatives contributes to "shirking" behavior. Shirking occurs when members take actions that do not contribute to the maximum efficiency of the organization.[66] Shirking may arise, for example, when a fighter takes a nap instead of setting up a roadside bomb to attack a government convoy. Or, alternatively, a fighter may wantonly kill civilians in ways that undermine local support for the organization. With no one around to monitor behavior, the fighter may calculate that he will not be caught. An organization's success depends on its ability to motivate members and encourage them to behave in ways consistent with its broader goals and objectives. A lack of discipline among lower-ranking members can waste resources, alienate potential supporters, and undermine military and political efforts. Leaders need to make decisions about how to shape, manage, and control the behavior of their members.[67]

There are other potential explanations for al Qa'ida's decentralization, though most are problematic. It is possible, for example, that al Qa'ida leaders and other Salafi jihadists increasingly believe that a diffuse structure is more effective in trying to achieve their objectives. Decentralized groups can be more adaptive and resilient in conducting operations.[68] Some Salafi jihadists encouraged a decentralized structure. One was the Syrian jihadist thinker Abu Mus'ab al-Suri, whose work was widely circulated on jihadist websites. He encouraged Muslims to become involved in "individual jihad and small cell terrorism."[69] A decentralized strategy, he argued, is more likely to be successful in conducting disparate, hit-and-run, guerrilla-style attacks against better armed government forces. As Suri concluded: "The jihad of individual or cell terrorism, using the methods of urban or rural guerilla warfare, is fundamental for exhausting the enemy and causing him to collapse and withdraw."[70] A range of terrorist and insurgent groups have adopted decentralized strategies. In the United States, for example, anti-government activist and white supremacist Louis Beam advocated an organizational structure, which he termed "leaderless resistance," to target the U.S. government. As Beam noted: "Utilizing the Leaderless Resistance concept, all individuals and groups operate independently of each other, and never report to a central headquarters or single leader for direction or instruction, as would those who belong to a typical pyramid organization."[71] In addition, a range of left-wing revolutionaries, radicals, and anarchists have adopted networked organizational structures.[72]

While some Salafi-jihadist leaders have encouraged a decentralized movement, including for al Qa'ida and its affiliates, this shift appears to be a *result* of other factors, such as successful counterterrorism efforts by the United States and other governments. In addition, there is little evidence that al Qa'ida's leaders, including Osama bin

Laden, actively supported a decentralized strategy if it meant losing control and influence over affiliates.

A Growing Vulnerability

The decentralized structure of al Qa'ida and other Salafi-jihadist groups should be a cause of concern for its leaders, and it presents an opportunity for counterterrorism agencies. Decentralized groups have a low probability of achieving their objectives. Among the roughly 180 insurgencies since World War II, several of which al Qa'ida and other Salafi-jihadist groups participated in, there has been substantial variation in the degree of centralization among groups. Some groups have enjoyed a high level of central control (the leadership directly controls virtually all operations and resources); others have a moderate level of central control (the leadership directly controls some, but not all, operations and resources); and still others have a low level of centralized control (the leadership directly controls few operations and resources).[73] Groups with high levels of centralization have been more likely to achieve victory (41.5 percent) than ones with moderate levels (31.4 percent) or low levels (17.4 percent) of centralization.[74] It is not entirely clear why high levels of centralization are more strongly correlated with insurgent victory, since numerous factors impact the outcome of insurgencies.[75]

But the cold reality for al Qa'ida and Salafi-jihadist groups is that decentralized groups are unlikely to succeed in achieving their long-term objectives. Decentralized groups are more likely to face principal-agent problems, and they may also find it challenging to control territory, since lower-levels cells are more likely to usurp power and resources for their own interests with limited oversight. Finally, there is often a higher likelihood of divisions among decentralized groups and movements, making it easier for government agencies to play groups against each other and sow discord among them.

Consequently, the decentralized nature of al Qa'ida and other Salafi-jihadist groups will likely present growing problems. As core al Qa'ida leaders in Pakistan wrote in a February 2014 letter rebuking the Islamic State of Iraq and al-Sham, "We emphasize our disavowal from the sedition that is occurring in al-Sham from the factions of the mujahideen, and our disavowal from the forbidden blood that was shed by any party." They then warned Muslims worldwide to recognize "the enormity of the disaster that afflicted the Jihad in Syria and the future of the Muslim Ummah with the sedition they are experiencing."[76]

CHAPTER THREE

Growing Capabilities

In September 2013, al Shabaab operatives grabbed international headlines by conducting a deadly attack at the upscale Westgate Mall in Nairobi, Kenya, killing at least 59 people and wounding nearly 200 others. The attackers carefully selected the Westgate Mall among possible alternatives; conducted intelligence, surveillance, and reconnaissance; moved operatives and equipment into place; performed rehearsals; executed the attack; and implemented an information campaign before, during, and after the attack.[1] During the attack, they utilized Twitter to update followers and orchestrate a propaganda campaign. Two months after the operation, al Shabaab released a special edition of its magazine, *Gaidi Mtaani*, devoted to the mall attack. The magazine justified the attack as retaliation for Kenya's alleged "blatant aggression against Islam and Muslims," as well as Kenya's purported "blind and aimless bombardment of civilians by Kenyan jets and ships."[2] Al Shabaab pulled off the attack despite losing as much as 85 percent of the territory it controlled in 2010 in Somalia. More broadly, the Westgate Mall attack triggered a re-examination of the threat from Salafi-jihadist groups.

In light of this and other developments, this chapter asks several questions. How have the size and capabilities of Salafi-jihadist groups evolved over time—and why? To answer these questions, this chapter examines both quantitative and qualitative data. In particular, it analyzes a database of Salafi-jihadist groups, fighters, and levels of violence to assess recent trends and comes to several conclusions.

First, the number of Salafi-jihadist groups and fighters has grown over the past several years, particularly in North Africa and the Levant. Examples include groups operating in such countries as Tunisia, Algeria, Mali, Libya, Egypt (including the Sinai Peninsula), Lebanon, and Syria. Second, there has been an increase in the number of attacks perpetrated by al Qa'ida, especially by al Qa'ida in the Arabian Peninsula, the Islamic State of Iraq and al-Sham (which eventually broke with al Qa'ida), al Shabaab, and Jabhat al-Nusrah. Third, not all of these groups threaten the United States or other Western countries. Some groups, such as al Qa'ida in the Arabian Peninsula, have plotted attacks against the U.S. homeland. Others, such as Ansar al-Sharia Libya and al Shabaab, have planned attacks against U.S. embassies and citizens overseas. Others have been focused exclusively on local regimes. This increase in Salafi-jihadist groups has likely been caused by weakening governance across North Africa and the Middle East, as well as the expansion of Salafi-jihadist operatives that have spent time at terrorist training camps, fought on jihadist battlefields, or been released or escaped from prison.

Number and Size of Groups

While Salafi-jihadist groups have decentralized over the past decade, there was a notable increase in the number of groups after 2010. Figure 3.1 shows the number of Salafi-jihadist groups active by year since 1988 from our database. Each data point on the y-axis represents the number of active Salafi-jihadist groups that year. As highlighted in the figure, there was a steady increase in the number of groups during the 1990s and 2000s, but a notable jump in the slope of the line after 2010. The number of Salafi-jihadist groups in 2013 marked a 58-percent increase from the number in 2010. Virtually all of these Salafi-jihadist groups were in North Africa (such as Ansar al-Sharia Libya and the Muhammad Jamal Network) and the Levant (such as Jabhat al-Nusrah and Liwa al-Islam).

Figure 3.2 provides a rough estimate of the number of Salafi-jihadist fighters between 1988 and 2013, based on our database. Cal-

Figure 3.1
Number of Salafi-Jihadist Groups by Year, 1988–2013

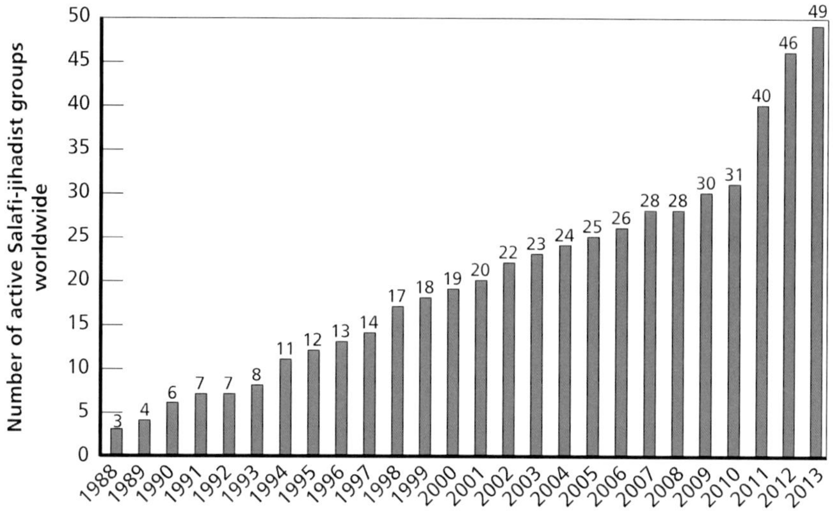

RAND *RR637-3.1*

Figure 3.2
Number of Salafi-Jihadists by Year, 1988–2013

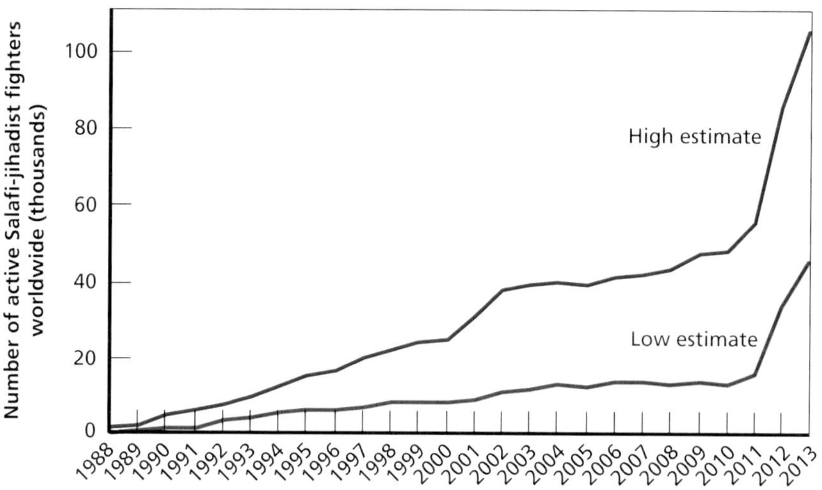

RAND *RR637-3.2*

culating the number of Salafi jihadists is difficult, in part since groups do not provide public estimates of their numbers and they can vary considerably over the course of a group's life. In fact, some groups may not have precise estimates of their own fighters because of fluctuations in numbers. Consequently, Figure 3.2 includes high and low estimates for the number of Salafi jihadists by year. The trend is similar to Figure 3.1. The number of Salafi jihadists more than doubled between 2010 and 2013, based on high and low estimates.[3] The biggest jump was in Syria, which witnessed a dramatic rise in the number of fighters. By early 2014, Salafi-jihadist groups represented a significant portion of the Syrian rebel manpower, including Jabhat al-Nusrah (2,000–6,000 fighters), Islamic State of Iraq and al-Sham (1,000–5,000 in Syria), Suqour al-Sham (2,000–5,000), Ahrar al-Sham (10,000–15,000), Liwa al-Islam (5,000–10,000), and Liwa al-Tawhid (5,000–10,000).[4]

Several examples highlight the surge in new Salafi-jihadist groups after 2010 in North Africa and the Levant. In Egypt, Muhammad Jamal established a Salafi-jihadist organization in 2011 following the overthrow of President Hosni Mubarak. Jamal had trained in al Qa'ida camps in Afghanistan in the late 1980s and returned to Egypt in the 1990s to become a top military commander for Egyptian Islamic Jihad, headed at the time by Ayman al-Zawahiri. After his release from an Egyptian prison in 2011, Muhammad Jamal took advantage of a permissive environment within Egypt following Mubarak's resignation, a network of militants he developed before and during his time in prison, and a relationship with leaders from al Qa'ida in the Islamic Maghreb and al Qa'ida in the Arabian Peninsula. Jamal, who was captured again in 2013, and his group have been committed to attacking targets in Egypt and the region, including U.S. and Western targets.[5] There has also been a rise in the number of Salafi-jihadist groups in the Sinai in Egypt, particularly Ansar Bayt al-Maqdis and the Mujahidin Shura Council, which have conducted attacks against the Egyptian government and Israel. Both are Salafi-jihadist groups dedicated to implementing *shari'a* in areas they control.[6]

Libya experienced a rise in the number of Salafi-jihadist groups after the overthrow of Muammar Qaddafi, making it perhaps the most active Salafi-jihadist sanctuary in North Africa. By the early 2000s,

Qaddafi's regime had effectively targeted terrorist groups in Libya. Indeed, Secretary of State Condoleezza Rice praised Qaddafi in 2006 for the "tangible results that flow from the historic decisions taken by Libya's leadership in 2003 to renounce terrorism and to abandon its weapons of mass destruction programs."[7] While Qaddafi's overthrow and the July 2012 democratic elections represented a remarkable achievement for political freedom, Libya has faced significant governance challenges. The bureaucracy is weak; well-armed militias control much of the countryside; and Salafi-jihadist groups attacked Sufi shrines across the country, digging up graves and destroying mosques and libraries.

The establishment of Ansar al-Sharia Libya highlights the emergence of Salafi jihadists in the country. Ansar al-Sharia Libya is a loose collection of militants based out of such cities as Benghazi, Darnah, and Misratah that seeks to establish *shari'a* in the country.[8] It comprises former rebels from the Abu Obayda Bin Aljarah Brigade, Malik Brigade, February 17 Brigade, and other militias bolstered by the 2011 overthrow of Qaddafi. Its first major public appearance occurred in June 2012, when leaders orchestrated a rally of armed vehicles along Benghazi's Tahrir Square and demanded the imposition of *shari'a*. Their nominal leader, Muhammad Ali al-Zahawi, remarked that "our brave youths will continue their struggle until they impose *shari'a*."[9] Over the past year, Ansar al-Sharia operatives in Benghazi worked to portray themselves as a local movement to garner popular support by providing security at a local hospital, publicizing their charity work, and using slogans such as "Your Sons at Your Service."[10] In addition to Ansar al-Sharia Libya, several other Salafi-jihadist groups enjoy a sanctuary in Libya: the Muhammad Jamal Network, which established a presence in such northern areas as Benghazi and Darnah; Mokhtar Belmokhtar's al-Murabitun in the southwest around Ghat, Awbari, and Tasawah; al Qa'ida in the Islamic Maghreb in parts of southwestern and northeastern Libya; and Ansar al-Sharia Tunisia in such areas as Darnah and Ajdabiya.

Elsewhere in North Africa, Mokhtar Belmokhtar's al-Murabitun established a presence in an arc of territory that includes Algeria, Libya, Mali, Niger, and Mauritania. During the fall of 2012, Belmokhtar announced that he split from al Qa'ida in the Islamic Maghreb to prioritize attacks against Western interests.[11] He also became involved in an ideological and leadership struggle with al Qa'ida in the Islamic Maghreb leader Abdelmalek Droukdal. In January 2013, his group participated in the attack against a multinational gas facility in In-Amenas, Algeria. In August 2013, Belmokhtar rebranded his group al-Murabitun and he envisions a unified North African jihadist front.[12] Other groups, including al Qa'ida in the Islamic Maghreb, retain a presence in southern Algeria, including around Tamanrasset, as well as in northern Algeria along the Mediterranean coast.

In Tunisia, Sayfallah Ben Hassine (also known as Abu Ayadh al-Tunisi) established Ansar al-Sharia Tunisia in 2011. The group has partnered with al Qa'ida in the Islamic Maghreb to target Western interests. Hassine aspires to become al Qa'ida's emir in Tunisia and plotted an attack in September 2012 against the U.S. embassy in Tunis. Ansar al-Sharia held a national conference at Kairouan in 2012 called for the Islamization of Tunisia's media, education, tourism and commercial sectors. It also advocated the establishment of an Islamic trade union to confront the secular Tunisian General Labor Union.[13] The group, which is a loose collection of networks, also uses Libya as a safe haven. In August 2013, Tunisian authorities declared Ansar al-Sharia Tunisia a terrorist organization.[14]

In Mali, Iyad ag Ghali founded Harakat Ansar-al Din in late 2011. The group developed close ties to al Qa'ida in the Islamic Maghreb, which it leveraged in cooperating with local Mali groups in the capture of the Malian towns of Agulhok, Tessalit, Kidal, Gao, and Timbuktul in early 2012.[15] But the group suffered a significant setback in 2013, when French and Malian forces retook most of these areas during Operation Serval.

In Nigeria, Abubakar Shekau emerged as one of the most dangerous extremist figures in West Africa, asserting leadership over Nigeria's radical Islamic sect, Boko Haram, and rebranding it as a regional jihadist enterprise. Motivated to avenge the alleged oppression of Muslims by the Nigerian government and its Western allies, Shekau and his group amassed weapons, improved their capabilities, and secured funding, training, and resources from other terrorist organizations.[16]

By 2014, more than 3 million people in Nigeria faced a humanitarian crisis because of the Boko Haram–led insurgency.[17]

Figure 3.3 highlights the locations of several Salafi-jihadist groups in Libya, while Figure 3.4 highlights the locations of such groups in the Middle East. Many of these groups have engaged in joint training, exchanged information, and occasionally conducted joint operations. In addition, virtually every group highlighted in Figures 3.3 and 3.4 has a presence in more than one country, suggesting that there is

Figure 3.3
Areas of Salafi-Jihadist Activity in Libya, 2014

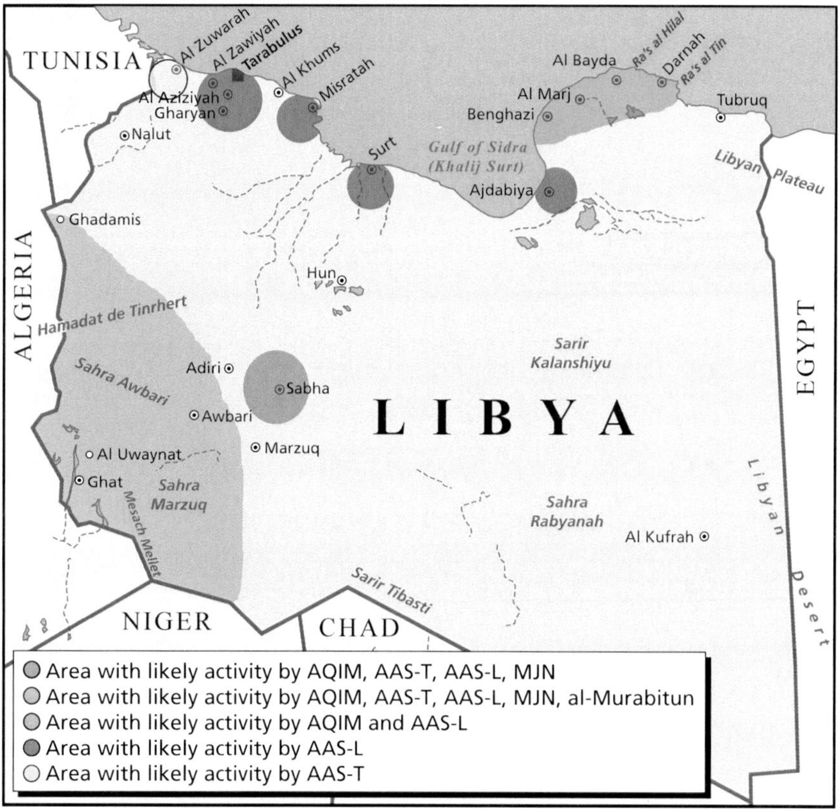

NOTE: AQIM = Al Qa'ida in the Islamic Maghreb, AAS-L = Ansar al-Sharia Libya, AAS-T = Ansar al-Sharia Tunisia, MJN = Muhammad Jamal Network.

RAND *RR637-3.3*

Figure 3.4
Location of Selected Salafi-Jihadist Groups in the Middle East, 2014

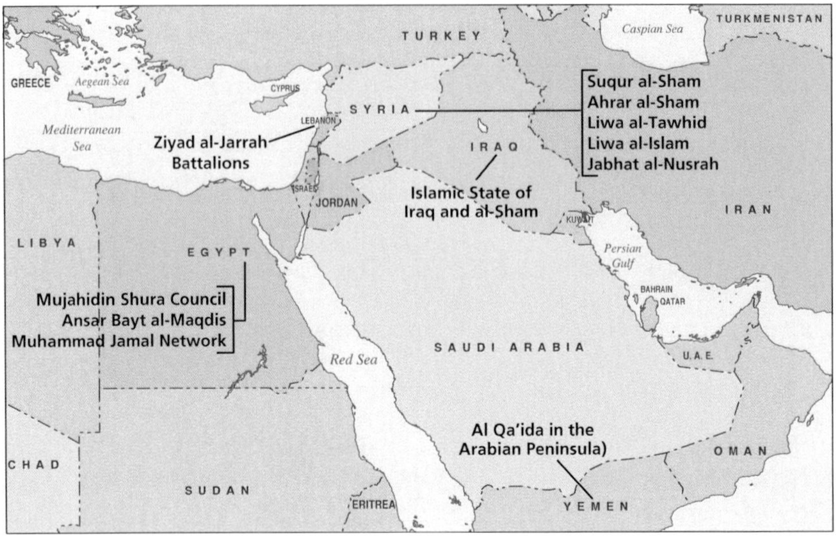

RAND *RR637.3.4*

considerable intra-group (as well as inter-group) movement in fighters, money, weapons, and other resources across national boundaries. Perhaps most concerning is that Libya has become a sanctuary for multiple Salafi-jihadist groups, which have used its territory for training and rearming.

Since 2011, there has also been a significant increase in the number of groups in the Levant, especially in Syria. The insurgency in Syria has acted as a magnet for Salafi-jihadist and other Islamist groups. In June 2013, for example, leading Sunni religious scholars in Egypt issued a fatwa declaring that it is a religious obligation for all Muslims to provide human, financial, and material support to the Syrian opposition.[18] Salafi-jihadist groups have benefited, growing in influence and size. By early 2014, these groups represented a significant portion of the Syrian rebel manpower compared to 2012, when Salafi jihadists represented less than one quarter of the rebel population, and from 2011, when there were virtually no Salafi-jihadist groups in Syria.[19] There has also been an increase of Salafi-jihadist groups in Lebanon, including the Ziyad al-Jarrah Battalions, which began operating around 2009.[20]

Some analysts have tried to measure the area of control or influence by Salafi-jihadist groups.[21] However, the data appear far too unreliable to make a quantitative judgment, especially changes over time. Still, the growth in the number and size of Salafi-jihadist groups suggests that Salafi jihadists may control more territory today than prior to the Arab uprisings. This has likely been true for some groups, such as Jabhat al-Nusrah, which did not exist before 2011. As Figure 3.5 highlights, Jabhat al-Nusrah has been active in several areas of Syria. Its most secure sanctuary is likely in the Sunni-dominated Dayr az-Zawr province, where al Qa'ida in Iraq's foreign fighter pipeline operated for nearly a decade. A second area is in northwestern Syria, where Jabhat

Figure 3.5
Areas of Jabhat al-Nusrah Activity in Syria, 2014

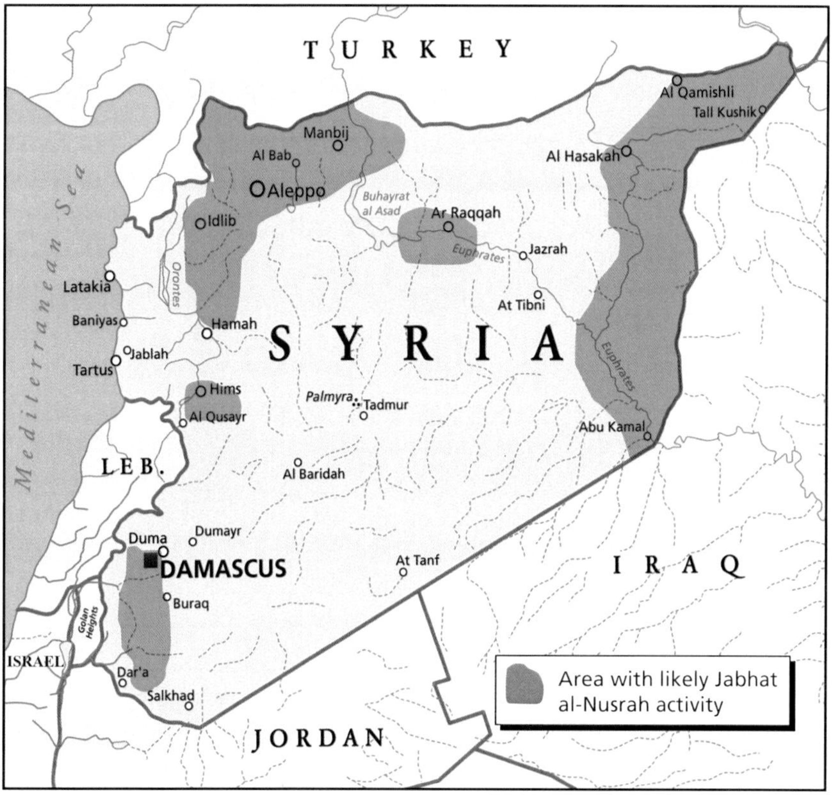

RAND *RR637-3.5*

al-Nusrah has moved fighters, explosives, and other material across the Turkish border into its sanctuaries in Halab and Idlib provinces. Reminiscent of groups like Hezbollah, Jabhat al-Nusrah has set up some humanitarian relief efforts in these provinces, along with religious courts and schools. Jabhat al-Nusrah has also established a sanctuary in southwestern Syria in Dar'a province, near the Jordanian border, as well as in Damascus.[22] Jabhat al-Nusrah has imposed *shari'a* in some areas that it controls, such as in Mayadin.[23]

Capabilities and Levels of Violence

In light of the growing number of Salafi-jihadist groups and fighters, this section turns to trends in violence.

Core al Qa'ida and Affiliates

We begin with core al Qa'ida and its affiliates. Figure 3.6 highlights the number of attacks by core al Qa'ida and affiliates since 2007.[24] The data indicate a substantial rise in the number of attacks over time. Trends for casualties and fatalities were similar. There was a significant increase in attacks by al Qa'ida–affiliated groups between 2007 and 2013, with most of the violence in 2013 perpetrated by the Islamic State of Iraq and al-Sham (43 percent), al Shabaab (25 percent), Jabhat al-Nusrah (21 percent), and al Qa'ida in the Arabian Peninsula (10 percent). This marked a change from 2012, when al Shabaab conducted the largest percentage of attacks (46 percent).

The data show that violence levels are highest in Yemen, Somalia, Iraq, and Syria. These attacks also include a mixture of suicide attacks, complex attacks using multiple individuals and cells, assassinations, and various types of improvised explosive devices against local government targets and civilians. Figure 3.7 highlights the number of attacks against the far enemy, near enemy, or a combination of both between 2007 and 2013.[25] Approximately 99 percent of al Qa'ida and affiliated attacks in 2013 were against near-enemy targets, the highest percentage of attacks against the near enemy in a single year in our database. This suggests that al Qa'ida and its affiliates have deliberately chosen to

Figure 3.6
Number of Attacks by al Qa'ida and Affiliates, 2007–2013

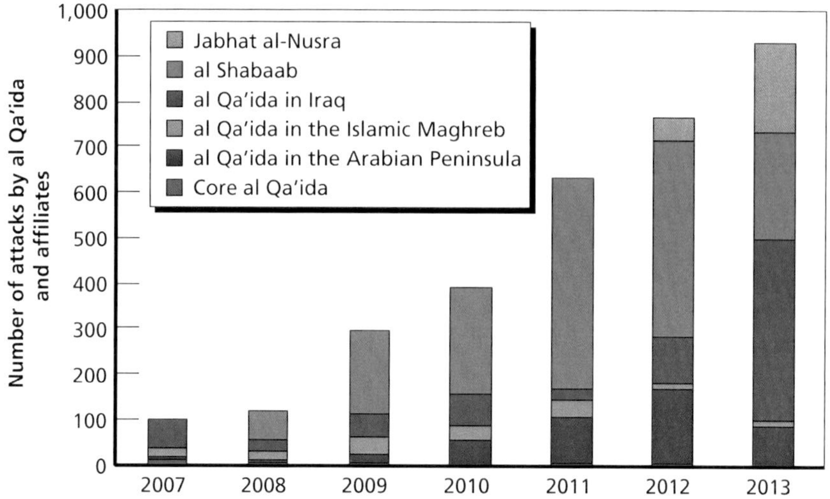

SOURCE: Data are based on author estimates and the Jane's Terrorism and Insurgency Intelligence Centre Events Database.
RAND *RR637-3.6*

focus on the near enemy for the moment, found it increasingly difficult to strike far-enemy targets, or a combination of both.

These trends in attacks are similar to patterns in both casualties and fatalities. The highest levels were perpetrated by al Qa'ida in the Arabian Peninsula, the Islamic State of Iraq and al-Sham, al Shabaab, and Jabhat al-Nusrah.

In Yemen, al Qa'ida in the Arabian Peninsula retains a sanctuary in several governorates, including in southern Hadramawt, Shabwah, and Abyan along the Gulf of Aden, as well as around such cities as Rada' (in Al Bayda' governorate), Sana'a (Sana'a), Wadi Abidah (Ma'rib), and Yatamah (Al Jawf). The group has demonstrated an ability to mount large-scale, mass-casualty attacks across Yemen, especially in southern Yemen. Al Qa'ida in the Arabian Peninsula has also benefited from limited Yemeni government operations. Since mid-2012, President Abd Rabbuh Mansur Hadi has avoided sustained ground offensives in favor of air strikes and small-scale raids against al Qa'ida sanctuaries, perhaps to minimize government casualties. On September 20, 2013,

Figure 3.7
Far Enemy Versus Near Enemy Attacks by al Qa'ida and Affiliates, 2007–2013

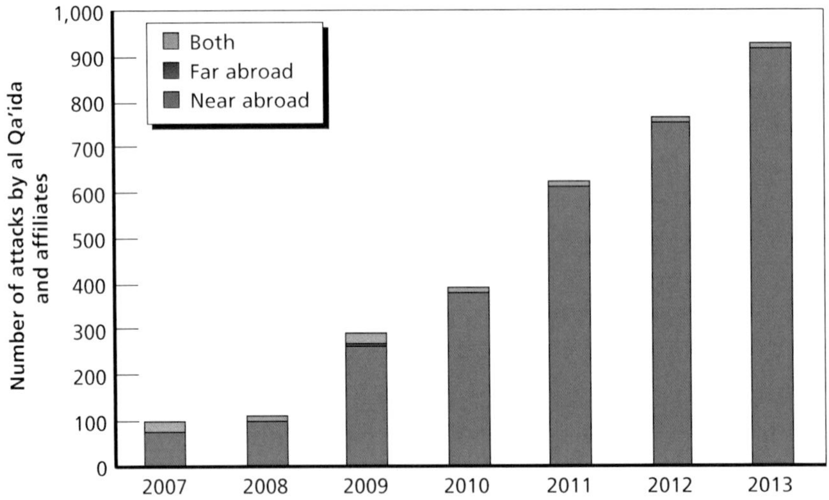

SOURCE: Data are based on author estimates and the Jane's Terrorism and Insurgency Intelligence Centre Events Database.
RAND *RR637-3.7*

al Qa'ida attacked military facilities in Shabwah governorate, killing as many as 56 Yemeni security personnel. On December 5, al Qa'ida operatives launched a complex attack against the Yemeni Ministry of Defense complex in Sana'a, killing 40 Yemeni personnel and civilians and wounding dozens more. They detonated a suicide vehicle bomb that breached a fence inside the compound, which allowed six or more militants to attack the military leadership hospital on the compound.[26]

In Somalia, al Shabaab has been involved in a series of attacks against the Transitional Federal Government and its supporters, particularly Kenya, Uganda, soldiers from the African Union Mission in Somalia (AMISOM), and pro-government militias. By early 2014, al Shabaab lost as much as 85 percent of the territory it controlled in 2010, including in Mogadishu and Kismaayo.[27] But it still conducted high-profile attacks in Somalia and neighboring countries, especially Kenya, using a combination of suicide operatives, assault teams, and improvised explosive devices. Al Shabaab claimed responsibility for two explosions on the Maka al-Mukarama Hotel in November 2013, located close to Somali government facilities. One of the bombings involved a laptop rigged with explosives.[28] Al Shabaab has apparently explored the possibility of concealing bombs inside consumer electronic items, such as laptop computers, cameras, and tape recorders. More broadly, al Shabaab has targeted Somali government officials and structures in Somalia (such as the head of the Somali National Intelligence and Security Agency, other security officials, and members of parliament), foreigners in Somalia (such as United Nations officials and AMISOM forces), government targets in the region (such as the Kenyan Parliament), and civilians in the region (such as the Westgate Mall in Nairobi).[29]

In Iraq, the Islamic State of Iraq and al-Sham has significantly increased its attack tempo since 2011, focusing on Shi'a and Iraqi government targets. In fact, the group has likely targeted more Shi'a than every other al Qa'ida affiliate *combined*.[30] By 2013, attacks by the Islamic State of Iraq and al-Sham had surpassed levels in 2011, the last year that U.S. military forces were in Iraq, and controlled small amounts of territory in areas like Fallujah in Al-Anbar Province. Most were vehicle-bomb attacks, with smaller numbers of suicide attacks. In neighboring Syria, the Islamic State of Iraq and al-Sham's seizure of weapons and money from Syrian rebel groups, execution of some rebel leaders, and refusal to participate in peace talks triggered a backlash. Several groups, including the Islamic Front, Syrian Revolutionary Front, and even Jabhat al-Nusrah engaged in heavy fighting with the Islamic State of Iraq and al-Sham.

Jabhat al-Nusrah amassed an impressive arsenal of weapons, making it one of al Qa'ida's best-armed affiliates in the world. It participated with other groups in seizing control of several Syrian military bases and acquired a vast array of armaments—including heavy artillery, machine guns, rocket-propelled grenades, and aircraft—to enhance its firepower. Indeed, Jabhat al-Nusrah's capabilities are more akin to a small army than a rag-tag group of guerrilla fighters. In February 2013, Jabhat al-Nusrah fighters helped seize control of the al-Jarrah airbase in Thawra, as well as two dams in Raqqa.[31] A video released on YouTube of Islamist fighters battling Syrian forces at the al-Jarrah airbase showed aircraft in hangars. In January, Jabhat al-Nusrah and Ahrar al-Sham teamed up with the Islamic Vanguard to seize control of Taftanaz, a key Syrian Air Force base in Idlib. In December 2012, Jabhat al-Nusrah and allied groups took control of the Sheikh Suleiman base. In October, Jabhat al-Nusrah and allied fighters overran a Syrian air defense and Scud missile base in Aleppo.[32] Jabhat al-Nusrah also seized military bases with other groups, including the Salafi-jihadist Suqur al-Sham.

Core al Qa'ida, however, has been involved in few attacks and plots, a dramatic drop-off from a decade ago. One of the last advanced core al Qa'ida plots was in 2009, when Najibullah Zazi planned suicide attacks against targets in New York City. The data compiled for this report suggest that the number of terrorist plots attempted by Islamic extremists against the U.S. homeland since 9/11 has been relatively small: ten known plots in 2009, seven in 2010, nine in 2011, six in 2012, and two in 2013. This data should be taken with caution, however. There may be some plots that remain classified by U.S. government agencies, and raw numbers do not indicate the severity of the plots or the degree of threat posed by individuals arrested.

In North Africa, al Qa'ida in the Islamic Maghreb has been involved in fewer attacks than other al Qa'ida affiliates. But it has covered a broader region than most affiliates, plotting attacks and kidnappings in Mali, Tunisia, Algeria, Morocco, and other countries in North Africa. The group has funded itself, in part, through kidnappings. In October 2013, for instance, al Qa'ida in the Islamic Maghreb received nearly $30 million for releasing four French hostages.[33]

Other Salafi Jihadists

Several other Salafi-jihadist groups have been active. One is Boko Haram, which has spearheaded an insurgency against the Nigerian government, based out of such northern states as Borno, Yobe, Kano, Kaduna, and Sokoto. It has been involved in an increasingly sophisticated campaign using suicide attacks, bombings, and assassinations against Nigerian government officials, Christian sites, and other government and civilian targets.[34] In 2014, Boko Haram operatives kidnapped more than 250 schoolgirls in an incident that gained worldwide attention. Boko Haram has benefited from training with al Qa'ida in the Islamic Maghreb and other militant groups, including in Mali.[35] It has leveraged networks in the Sahel and Central Africa and relied on facilitators, weapons dealers, and terrorist associates outside Nigeria to help conduct attacks and bolster its weapon stockpiles. In June 2013, Boko Haram members worked with associates of Mokhtar Belmokhtar to free several Boko Haram and al Qa'ida–linked extremists from prison in Niger.[36]

In Egypt, Ansar Bayt al-Maqdi and Mujahidin Shura Council have conducted attacks against Israel and the Egyptian government. Ansar Bayt al-Maqdi claimed responsibility for numerous attacks in Egypt since President Muhammad Morsi's ouster and has conducted assassinations and remotely detonated improvised explosive devices against Egyptian security forces.[37] The Mujahidin Shura Council has claimed responsibility for nearly all of the rocket attacks against Israel emanating from the Gaza Strip and the Sinai Peninsula since March 2013. Following the Egyptian military coup d'etat in July 2013, Egyptian security forces have conducted a series of arrests and attacks against Salafi-jihadist groups in the Sinai Peninsula and in Egypt, including the Muhammad Jamal Network. In August 2013, for example, Egyptian services arrested Ayman al-Zawahiri's brother, Muhammad al-Zawahiri. The Muhammad Jamal Network has been involved in several notable attacks since its establishment. Some members of the organization were likely involved in the 2012 attacks against U.S. facilities in Benghazi, Libya, which led to the death of U.S. Ambassador Christopher Stevens. In addition, a Muhammad Jamal Network leader played a key role in planning and recruiting for the January 2013 attack at the In-Amenas gas facility in Algeria. Over the past year, however, the network has been weakened by the arrest of several senior leaders, including Muhammad Jamal, by Egyptian security services.[38]

In the North Caucasus, Salafi-jihadist groups like the Imarat Kavkaz continue to wage a low-level insurgency against Russia and were involved in plots against the 2014 Sochi Winter Olympics.[39] In South and Central Asia, a range of groups—such as the Islamic Movement of Uzbekistan, Islamic Jihad Union, and Lashkar-e-Taiba—remain active. Several of these groups, including Lashkar-e-Taiba, present a broader threat and continue to plot attacks in such countries as India. In Southeast Asia, a number of Salafi-jihadist groups retain capabilities. Abu Sayyaf, Jemaah Islamiya, and Khalifa Islamiya Mindanao operate in the Philippines, though they have been weakened by local counterterrorist operations. Jemaah Ansharut Tauhid, founded in 2008 by Abu Bakar Bashir, is Indonesia's most active Salafi-jihadist group. In North Africa, a range of Salafi-jihadist groups—such as al-Murabitun, Ansar al-Sharia Tunisia, and Ansar al-Sharia Libya—have plotted and orchestrated attacks. Most have been against local targets, though operatives affiliated with Ansar al-Sharia Libya have plotted attacks and kidnappings against Americans and other Westerners in Libya.

Varied Threat to the U.S. Homeland

While the Salafi-jihadist movement has become increasingly decentralized—including al Qa'ida—there has been an increase in the number and size of Salafi-jihadist groups, as well as an increase in the number of their attacks. Still, not all Salafi-jihadist groups present a direct threat to the United States and the West. This report divides Salafi-jihadist groups into three categories: those that pose a high threat because they are involved in active plotting against the U.S. homeland; those that pose a medium threat because they are involved in plotting attacks against U.S. facilities, such as embassies, and U.S. citizens overseas; and those that pose a low threat because they are focused on targeting local regimes or other countries (see Table 3.1).

The highest threat likely comes from al Qa'ida in the Arabian Peninsula, which retains a capability and desire to target the U.S. homeland and U.S. interests overseas. Several Yemen-based operatives—such as leader Nasir al-Wuhayshi, senior military commander Qasim al-Rimi, and senior official Ibrahim al-Banna—continue to support attacks against the United States. Core al Qa'ida also presents a threat because of its interest in targeting the U.S. home-

Table 3.1
Examples of Salafi-Jihadist Groups That Threaten the United States

	High Threat	Medium Threat	Low Threat
Characteristics	Active plotting against the U.S. homeland and U.S. targets overseas (e.g., U.S. embassies and citizens)	Active plotting against U.S. targets overseas (e.g., U.S. embassies and citizens)	Limited or no active plotting against U.S. targets overseas
Examples	• Al Qa'ida in the Arabian Peninsula • Core al Qa'ida • Some inspired individuals and networks	• Al Shabaab • Ansar al-Sharia Libya • Muhammad Jamal Network • Al Qa'ida in the Islamic Maghreb	• East Turkestan Islamic Movement • Suqor al-Sham

land, led by individuals such as Abdullah al-Shami. But core al Qa'ida leaders have had difficulty recruiting—or even inspiring—competent operatives in the West.[40] In an effort to reach out to Western jihadis, the first edition in 2014 of core al Qa'ida's magazine, *Resurgence*, was dedicated to radicalizing Westerners and encouraging independent attacks in the West. A small number of inspired individuals, like the Tsarnaev brothers, who perpetrated the April 2013 Boston Marathon bombings, also pose a threat. The growth in social media and the terrorist use of chat rooms, Facebook, Twitter, YouTube, and other sites has facilitated radicalization inside the United States.

Several Salafi-jihadist groups pose a medium-level threat because of their willingness and capability to target U.S. citizens and installations overseas. Ansar al-Sharia Tunisia, for instance, has planned attacks against U.S. diplomats and infrastructure in Tunis, including the U.S. embassy. Several groups with a presence in Libya—such as the various Ansar al-Sharia Libya groups and al Qa'ida in the Islamic Maghreb—also pose a threat. Al Shabaab's objectives are largely parochial, and it has conducted attacks in Somalia and the region. But al Shabaab possesses a competent external operations capability to strike targets outside of Somalia. The Westgate Mall attack was well planned and well executed, and involved sophisticated intelligence collection, surveillance, and reconnaissance of the target.[41] These skills could be used for other types of attacks directly targeting the United States and its citizens, particularly overseas. In addition, some Americans have traveled to Somalia over the past several years to fight for al Shabaab, though these numbers have apparently dropped in recent years.[42] Several al Shabaab leaders, including deputy leader Ma hat Karate and Jehad Serwan Mostafa (a U.S. citizen), have allegedly been interested in targeting Western and U.S. interests in the region.[43]

The Islamic State of Iraq and al-Sham, along with Jabhat al-Nusrah, are primarily interested in establishing Islamic emirates in Iraq, Syria, and the broader region. But the network of Salafi-jihadist groups in Syria, including Jabhat al-Nusrah, could pose a growing threat in the future. Jabhat al-Nusrah's access to foreign fighters, external networks in Europe and other areas, and bomb-making expertise suggest that it may already have the capability to plan, support, and conduct attacks against the West. There appears to be a growing contingent of foreign fighters—over 10,000—traveling to Syria to fight in the war. A significant number—perhaps 10 to 15 percent (roughly 1,000 to 1,500 fighters)—appear to be coming from Europe, especially from Belgium, France, and Sweden.[44] Security agencies from such European countries as France, Belgium, Germany, the Netherlands, the United Kingdom, and the Balkans have arrested fighters departing to, or returning from, Syria.

It is currently unclear whether most of these fighters will remain in Syria and other battlefields over the long run, move to other war zones such as North Africa, or return to the West. And even if some return, it is uncertain whether they will become involved in terrorist plots, focus on recruiting and fundraising, or become disillusioned with terrorism. Still, foreign fighters have historically been agents of instability. They can affect the conflicts they join, as they did in post-2003 Iraq by promoting sectarian violence and indiscriminate tactics. Perhaps more important, foreign fighter mobilizations empower transnational terrorist groups such as al Qa'ida, because volunteering for war is the principal stepping-stone for individual involvement in more extreme forms of militancy. When Muslims in the West radicalize, they usually do not plot attacks in their home country right away, but travel to a war zone first. A majority of al Qa'ida operatives began their militant careers as war volunteers, and most transnational jihadi groups today are by-products of foreign-fighter mobilizations.[45]

Finally, some Salafi-jihadist groups present a low-level threat to the United States. They do not possess the capability or intent to target the United States at home or overseas. They include such groups as the East Turkestan Islamic Movement, which is primarily interested in Chinese targets. Despite this categorization, there is some fluidity between levels. The Chechen group Imarat Kavkaz, led by Doku Umarov, posed a low-level threat to the United States, though its interest in targeting the 2014 Sochi Olympics raised the threat to U.S. citizens in the region.

Why the Expansion of Salafi-Jihadist Groups?

There are several reasons for the growth in Salafi-jihadist groups. First is the growing weakness of governments across Africa and the Middle East, which has created an opportunity for Salafi-jihadist groups to secure a foothold. The logic is straightforward: weak governments have difficulty establishing law and order, which permits militant groups and other substate actors to fill the vacuum.[46]

As used here, governance is defined as the set of institutions by which authority in a country is exercised.[47] It includes the ability to establish law and order, effectively manage resources, and implement sound policies. German sociologist Max Weber defined the state as "a human community that (successfully) claims the monopoly of the legitimate use of physical force within a given territory."[48] When state institutions are weak, opportunistic elements in society are able to take advantage.[49] State weakness is particularly likely in remote areas, where insurgent and terrorist groups can establish rural strongholds.[50] The more extreme the decline or absence of authority in a region, the more the population becomes "virgin territory" for those who would become an alternative government.[51] Weak governance fuels alternative power centers, and warlords often flourish.[52] Poor governance also increases the likelihood of insurgency and terrorism because the state's security forces are weak and lack popular legitimacy. These forces may be badly financed and equipped, organizationally inept, corrupt, politically divided, and poorly informed about events at the local level.[53]

A large body of quantitative evidence suggests that weak and ineffective governance is critical to the onset of substate actors—including insurgent and terrorist groups. One study, for example, analyzed 161 cases over a 54-year period and found that financially, organizationally, and politically weak central governments render insurgencies more feasible and attractive due to weak local policing or inept counterinsurgency practices.[54] The reverse is also true: strong governance decreases the probability of insurgency. In looking at 151 cases over a 54-year period, one study found that governance is critical to prevent insurgencies, arguing that success requires the "provision of temporary security, the building of new institutions capable of resolving future conflicts peaceably, and an economy capable of offering civilian employment to former soldiers and material progress to future citizens."[55] In addition, governmental capacity is a negative and significant predictor of civil war, and between 1816 and 1997 "effective bureaucratic and political systems reduced the rate of civil war activity."[56]

There are good reasons to believe that weak governance has contributed to the rise of Salafi-jihadist groups. Since 2010, a year before the Arab uprisings, there has been a significant weakening of governance across the Middle East and North Africa, according to World Bank data. Levels of political stability dropped by 17 percent from 2010 to 2012, government effectiveness by 10 percent, rule of law by 6 percent, and control of corruption by 6 percent across the Middle East and North Africa.[57] Of particular concern, governance deteriorated in numerous countries that saw a rise in Salafi-jihadist groups. Take rule of law, which includes the extent to which agents have confidence in and abide by the rules of society, particularly the quality of contract enforcement, property rights, the police, and the courts. Between 2010 and 2012, rule of law dropped by 21 percent in Egypt, 31 percent in Libya, 25 percent in Mali, 20 percent in Niger, 17 percent in Nigeria, 61 percent in Syria, and 39 percent in Yemen. To make matters worse, most of the countries had low levels of rule of law even before this drop.[58]

These data suggest that the decline in governance across the Middle East and North Africa may have contributed to the rise in Salafi-jihadist activity. Still, weak governance alone is not a sufficient explanation, since it cannot explain motivation (why certain groups filled the vacuum) or variation (why Salafi-jihadist groups took advantage of weak governance in North Africa, but not in, say, sub-Saharan Africa).

A second reason for the growth in Salafi-jihadist groups is the spread of militant networks. The logic is that operatives who have spent time training or fighting in countries such as Iraq, Afghanistan, and Pakistan have proactively moved to new countries in North Africa and the Levant. Individuals who spend time at training camps and fighting in jihadist battlefields generally establish trusted social relationships.[59] These conditions provide a unique environment for terrorists to pray together; share meals; train together in classrooms, at shooting ranges, and through physical conditioning; socialize with each other during breaks; and sometimes fight together. Camps and jihadist battlefields create and reinforce a shared religious identity and strategic culture dedicated to overthrowing infidel regimes.[60] For example, Umar Farouk Abdulmutallab, who attempted to blow up an airplane landing in Detroit on Christmas Day 2009, attended an al Qa'ida training camp in the Shabwah region of Yemen. There were over two-dozen fighters who dug trenches, crawled through barbed wire, and practiced tactical movements such as clearing buildings. The daily routine at the training camp consisted of rising early, praying, reading the Qur'an, completing warm-up drills, and conducting tactical training. After lunch, the students completed additional tactical training drills and stayed in tents at night.[61] The social interaction during daily routines experienced by individuals like Abdulmutallab creates a strong bond among operatives.

The syllabi in many of these camps and jihadist battlefields include theoretical and practical courses on weapons and explosives.[62] Individuals often study common religious texts, in addition to the Qur'an and the hadiths.[63] Testimonies of former fighters suggest the camps and battlefields can significantly improve the military capabilities of fighters, from building improvised explosive devices to honing counterintelligence practices and conducting complex attacks.[64] Participants also engage in *nasheeds*, or battle hymns sung a capella during training and socializing.[65] In short, the socialization process in camps, and later on the battlefield, develops and strengthens social and ideological bonds.

While there is limited data on foreign fighter flows, there is some evidence that individuals from al Qa'ida and other Salafi-jihadist camps and battlefronts have proactively migrated to the Middle East and North Africa to take advantage of governance vacuums.[66] In Syria, for example, Jabhat al-Nusrah leaders, including Abu Muhammad al-Jawlani, were veterans of the Iraq war and members of the Islamic State of Iraq and al-Sham. Mokhtar Belmokhtar, the emir of al-Murabitun, had spent time in al Qa'ida training camps in Afghanistan in the 1990s. In Egypt, Muhammad Jamal trained in Afghanistan in the late 1980s with al Qa'ida, where he learned to make bombs.[67] And Ma hat Karate, al Shabaab's deputy leader, trained in Afghanistan.

There are other possible explanations for the resurgence of Salafi jihadists, though most are problematic. One possibility is a rise in sectarian conflict between Sunnis and Shi'a, which may have contributed to a growth in resources available to Salafi-jihadist groups. Perhaps the most notable examples are in Iraq, Lebanon, and Syria. On one side are Sunni militants and their state backers from the Persian Gulf and other regions. On the other side are Shi'a groups like Hezbollah and their state supporters, especially Iran. It is possible that a growing sectarian struggle across the Middle East and North Africa has contributed to an increase in the number of groups that are flush with money, weapons, fighters, and other aid. Salafi-jihadist groups, then, may have benefited from Sunni state and non-state donors who were motivated to support them against Iran and other Shi'a.

One challenge with assessing this hypothesis, however, is that there is no comprehensive data on funding and other support to Salafi-jihadist groups, including for sectarian motivations. Still, there are good reasons to doubt this explanation. First, it does not account for the increase in Salafi-jihadist groups in North Africa, where there is little or no sectarian conflict because there are few Shi'a. Second, while Sunni groups in Syria, Iraq, and Lebanon have benefited from aid by outside actors inspired, in part, by sectarian motives, it is not clear how much outside funding has gone to Salafi-jihadist groups. Turkey, several Persian Gulf states, and Jordan have provided support to non–Salafi-jihadist groups in Syria. While Salafi-jihadist groups in the Levant have received some support from wealthy donors based on sectarian motives, it is unlikely that the increase in Salafi-jihadist groups across North Africa and the Levant is primarily caused by a sectarian struggle between Sunni and Shi'a. These arguments have also tended to overstate the degree of sectarian conflict, since there has been a substantial amount of intra-Sunni fighting across this region.

Another possibility is growing popular support for the Salafi-jihadist ideology. Perhaps populations across Africa and the Middle East have gravitated toward Salafi-jihadism, creating an opportunity for individuals to establish Salafi-jihadist groups. As previously noted, most Salafi jihadists believe that Islam today has become corrupt, and they support the use of armed jihad to establish a society based on an extreme interpretation of *shari'a*. Indeed, most Salafi jihadists emphasize the importance of *tawhid* and establishing *shari'a* in areas they control.

In the absence of reliable data on the number of Salafi-jihadist local supporters, it is difficult to entirely discount this argument. But there are good reasons to be skeptical that there has been an increase in support for Salafi-jihadism. Polling data indicate that support for Islamic extremist groups—including al Qa'ida—has *declined* in recent years in key parts of the Middle East and Africa. Support for al Qa'ida declined by 5 percent in Egypt from 2010 to 2013, 62 percent in Jordan, and 50 percent in Lebanon, according to data from the Pew Research Center. It also decreased by 6 percent in Tunisia between 2012 and 2013, and 63 percent in Nigeria between 2010 and 2013.[68] According to the same data, concerns about Islamic extremism were widespread across the Middle East and sub-Saharan Africa, with a median of 67 percent saying they are somewhat or very concerned about Islamic extremism.[69] Consequently, the available data cast considerable doubt that populations have become more supportive of Salafi-jihadism.

CHAPTER FOUR

Strategic Options

How should the United States respond to a diffuse yet spreading movement of Salafi-jihadist groups? Current trends suggest that the United States needs to remain focused on countering the proliferation of Salafi-jihadist groups in North Africa, the Middle East, and even South Asia, with the downsizing of U.S. military forces in Afghanistan. This is particularly important with the temptation to "rebalance" to the Asia-Pacific region and to decrease counterterrorism resources in a constrained fiscal environment. The U.S. Department of Defense's 2014 Quadrennial Defense Review, for example, bluntly noted that the United States should be "principally focused on preparing for the future by rebalancing our defense efforts in a period of increasing fiscal constraint." It also emphasized the importance of the Asia-Pacific region as "increasingly central to global commerce, politics and security."[1] Not surprisingly, much of the U.S. military—including the Army, Air Force, Navy, and Marine Corps—has shifted its attention to the Asia-Pacific theater, including such issues as force posture, acquisitions, campaign planning, and response to anti-access/area-denial (A2AD) challenges.

This shift is risky. For the near future, the most acute security threats to the U.S. homeland and its interests overseas will likely come from terrorist groups and state sponsors of terror, not countries in the Asia-Pacific. To complicate matters, most U.S. government agencies involved in counterterrorism have not systematically apportioned or adequately synchronized their declining resources to focus on the most serious threats. This chapter examines strategic options and provides a framework to help focus America's limited resources.

As used here, "strategy" refers to a plan to defeat or degrade terrorist groups.[2] Government officials need to consider how to use their military forces and other tools—including economic and diplomatic ones—to defeat or weaken groups.[3] While this chapter focuses on strategies to counter Salafi-jihadist groups, the conceptual approach could be used for countering terrorist groups more broadly.[4] Figure 4.1 provides a rough illustration of the strategic challenge. The y-axis measures the capacity of local governments to establish the rule of law in their countries, using data from the World Bank. The x-axis measures the threat to the United States, using author estimates.[5] The bottom right-hand quadrant of Figure 4.1 indicates the countries where there is a high terrorist threat and low government capacity. The data suggest that the most concerning countries for the United States include Afghanistan, Pakistan, and Yemen, where there is a high potential threat to the United States and limited local rule of law. There is another set of troubling countries in the lower right-hand quadrant—such as Somalia,

Figure 4.1
Countries of Concern for the United States

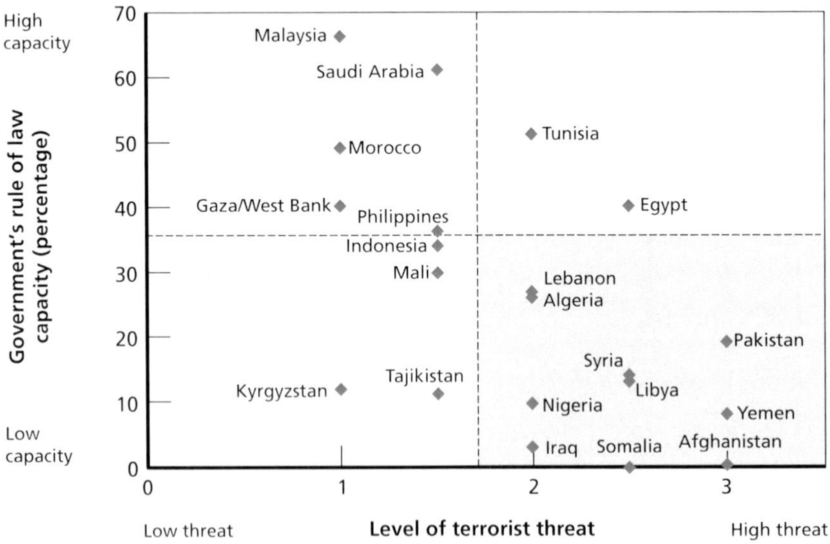

RAND *RR637-4.1*

Iraq, Syria, Libya—with a medium Salafi-jihadist threat to the United States (including to U.S. interests overseas) and weak local governance.

Viewed in this context, the chapter argues that at least two factors should impact U.S. counterterrorism strategy overseas against Salafi-jihadist groups: the threat by terrorists to the United States, and the capacity and political will of local governments to counter these groups.[6] First, the threat includes the interests and capabilities of a group to attack the United States at home and abroad. Does the group have a desire to plot attacks against the U.S. homeland or U.S. interests—such as embassies or other diplomatic missions—overseas? Does the group have the capability to conduct attacks, such as the technical proficiency to build bombs and move them to the target area, competent operatives who can carry out attacks (including in the United States), and intelligence collection and reconnaissance capabilities? Second, government capacity includes the ability or desire of the local government, including its security services, to counter groups operating on its soil. Examples of factors that contribute to government capacity include a high level of government initiative; sufficient intelligence; civil-military integration; competent leadership; and trained and motivated police, soldiers, and intelligence operatives.[7] It also includes the political will of the government to target Salafi-jihadist groups that threaten the United States. Some governments may focus on other internal or external threats they consider more pressing, and still others may be hostile to the United States.

Based on the threat to the United States and the capacity and will of the local government, the United States should pursue a mixture of three strategies: *engagement* where there is a threat to the United States and low government capacity or will; *forward partnering* where there is a threat to the United States but substantial local government capacity, or a growing threat but limited or no local capacity; and *offshore balancing* where there is a low threat to the United States and sufficient local government capacity or an ally (like a NATO country) willing to counter Salafi-jihadist groups. Table 4.1 provides a summary. These strategies are fleshed out in more detail in the rest of this chapter.

There are several additional strategies the United States could consider, though they are likely too risky. For example, the United States

Table 4.1
A Summary of Strategic Options

Strategy	Overview	Benefits	Risks
Engagement	• U.S. forces are directly involved in targeting terrorists • U.S. builds capacity of local governments	• Allows U.S. to deal directly with imminent terrorist threats • Prevents delegation of U.S. security to others • Keeps U.S. presence "limited" to clandestine U.S. agencies	• Could inflame local population and support terrorist narrative • Entails greater financial and human costs than the other two strategies • Raises risk of mission creep • Raises possibility of blowback
Forward Partnering	• U.S. builds capacity of local governments • U.S. forces are not directly involved in targeting terrorists	• Retains some U.S. influence through presence • Decreases likelihood of blowback • Lowers financial and human costs compared to engagement	• Risky in cases where a group is plotting attacks against U.S. • U.S. presence can still embolden terrorist narrative • Local government may be ineffective or unwilling to target groups
Offshore Balancing	• Little or no U.S. effort to build capacity • U.S. uses offshore air, naval, ground forces • U.S. forces are not directly involved in targeting terrorists	• Lowers financial and human costs compared to the other two strategies • Reduces potential for inflaming local populations • Preserves U.S. air, naval, and ground options for *in extremis* situations	• Limited or no U.S. influence • Risky in cases where a group is plotting attacks against U.S. • Would not necessarily undermine terrorist narrative, especially groups that consider America an enemy

could adopt a strategy of primacy and become involved in countering terrorists in most countries with Salafi-jihadist groups.[8] This might involve utilizing conventional forces, as the United States did in Iraq and Afghanistan. But a primacy strategy is expensive and bloody. It would likely increase the number of U.S. enemies, discourage allies from paying for their own defense by emboldening free-riding, and entangle the United States in unnecessary wars where there is no immediate national security interest—a classic moral hazard problem.[9] The United States could also adopt an isolationist strategy and withdraw all—or most—U.S. forces, leaving the job of countering Salafi-jihadist groups to allies and local governments. But this strategy would severely jeopardize U.S. national security, especially in cases where Salafi-jihadist groups overseas were actively plotting attacks against the United States.

Strategy 1: Engagement

Engagement entails the use of intelligence, law enforcement, and special operations forces to conduct precision targeting of groups and their financial, logistical, and political support networks. If there is support from the local government, it can also include training, advising, and assisting governments in their struggle against terrorism. Engagement could involve orchestrating covert raids to capture or kill terrorists, seize their supplies, and target their finances; conducting air strikes from drones, fixed-wing aircraft, and helicopters; overseeing psychological operations to undermine terrorist support; collecting and analyzing intelligence about terrorist groups (their networks, locations, capabilities, and intentions); and engaging with tribal and other local actors.[10] In countries that are hostile to the United States but have groups that pose a threat—such as Iran (where there are some al Qa'ida operatives) and Syria (where there are a range of Salafi-jihadist groups)—U.S. engagement may be limited to such options as covert action by intelligence operatives or special operations forces acting under Title 50 authority.[11]

But an engagement strategy is limited in the sense that the United States would not deploy large numbers of U.S. forces, particularly conventional forces. The U.S. deployment of conventional forces to fight terrorists overseas has generally been counterproductive.[12] In Iraq, for instance, the large U.S. presence contributed to radicalization. In general, large numbers of U.S. forces tend to facilitate Salafi-jihadist recruitment and propaganda efforts. Perhaps more importantly, most successful overseas operations against al Qa'ida operatives in the past decade—such as against Khalid Sheikh Mohammad in Pakistan in 2003, Abu Mus'ab al Zarqawi in Iraq in 2006, Osama bin Laden in Pakistan 2011, and Anwar al-Awlaki in Yemen in 2011—were perpetrated by clandestine U.S. intelligence units and special operations forces. And most of the terrorists involved in serious homeland plots after September 11, 2001—from José Padilla's plan to blow up apartment buildings in the United States and Nidal Malik Hasan's mass shooting at Fort Hood to Najibullah Zazi and Faisal Shahzad's respective plots to conduct terrorist attacks in New York City—were motivated, in part, by the deployment of large numbers of U.S. combat troops in Muslim countries and by a conviction, however erroneous, that Muslims were its helpless victims.[13]

Still, there are risks with an engagement strategy. First, direct U.S. engagement could embolden the narrative of Salafi-jihadist groups, who will invariably attempt to portray the conflict as one between Islam and infidel countries. Direct U.S. participation will likely become public, despite efforts to keep it clandestine. Some in the United States may also balk at direct engagement in a foreign war. Second, there are often greater financial costs with an engagement strategy than the other strategies examined here, and they put American soldiers and intelligence operatives at greater risk. Third, there is a potential for mission creep. In Afghanistan, for example, the United States gradually raised its military footprint from several hundred in 2001 to approximately 100,000 by 2010 and became increasingly involved in nation-building. Fourth, there is a potential for blowback. In cases where Salafi-jihadist groups are not interested in targeting the U.S. homeland or its embassies, U.S. strikes against the group could cause a change in their behavior. After the 2009 U.S. killing of Tehreek-e-Taliban Pakistan (TTP) leader Baitullah Mehsud, for example, the TTP became increasingly interested in targeting the United States. In May 2010, Faisal Shahzad attempted to detonate a car bomb in New York City's Times Square, after being trained by TTP leaders in Pakistan.

But the benefits of an engagement strategy outweigh the risks in most cases where Salafi-jihadist groups are *already* plotting attacks against the U.S. homeland and its interests overseas (such as U.S. embassies), especially where the local government has minimal capabilities or little political will to counter the groups. One example is Yemen, where al Qa'ida in the Arabian Peninsula has been involved in multiple plots against the U.S. homeland and U.S. embassies, but whose government is relatively weak and embroiled in several domestic insurgencies and political unrest. Beginning in the summer of 2012, Yemeni President Abd Rabbuh Mansur Hadi became increasingly cautious about conducting operations against al Qa'ida in the Arabian Peninsula to minimize government casualties. He avoided large-scale ground offensives in favor of air strikes against al Qa'ida safe havens, including its stronghold in Mahfad District, Abyan governorate. In addition, the Yemeni military was fraught with problems. Many rank-and-file Yemeni soldiers did not receive their full pay because of endemic corruption in the military, undermining the military's effectiveness in countering al Qa'ida.

In these cases, a U.S. failure to become directly engaged could severely jeopardize U.S. national security if a group were to strike the U.S. homeland or a U.S. embassy. The risks of not being engaged could be serious. American lives may be lost and there would likely be substantial political costs if Americans concluded that U.S. policymakers did not do enough to prevent an attack. Still, the possibility that direct U.S. engagement could inflame the local population suggests that U.S. policymakers should carefully weigh the type of engagement. In some cases, it might make sense to limit U.S. engagement or conduct covert action by intelligence operatives or special operations forces acting under Title 50 authority.

Strategy 2: Forward Partnering

Forward partnering involves deploying small numbers of U.S. military forces, intelligence operatives, diplomats, and other government personnel to train local security forces, collect intelligence, and undermine terrorist financing.[14] Unlike an engagement strategy, however, U.S. forces would not become directly involved in the war by conducting raids, drone strikes, or other operations that involve participation in the war. Instead, their focus is building the capacity of the local government. A number of countries threatened by Salafi-jihadist groups in North Africa, the Middle East, and South Asia could benefit from U.S. or other outside training and assistance.

But there are risks with a forward partnering strategy. First, local governments can be fickle and uncooperative. A government that is willing to target Salafi-jihadist groups at one point can change its assessment. Pakistan, for example, was more willing to target al Qa'ida operatives on its soil in the immediate aftermath of 9/11. A decade later, however, it focused on countering groups conducting attacks in Pakistan cities, such as the Tehreek-e-Taliban Pakistan, and regional adversaries like India. Governments can also collapse. Egyptian President Hosni Mubarak, whose regime effectively countered terrorist groups, was overthrown in 2011 during the Arab Spring uprisings. Second, even indirect U.S. participation risks emboldening the Salafi-jihadist narrative, though less so than a direct engagement strategy. Al Shabaab leaders consider Western citizens as *kuffar*, or apostates.[15] As one al Shabaab document noted, it is *halal* (lawful) to kill and rob non-Muslims: "Ethiopians, Kenyans, Ugandans and Burundians are just like the English and the French because they have invaded the Islamic country of Somalia and launched war on Islam and Muslims."[16] Third, combating terrorist and insurgent groups is difficult, especially in countries with weak governments. There is no guarantee that building the capacity of local partners will weaken or defeat terrorist groups. In the absence of limited direct participation, the United States may become vulnerable to terrorist attacks.

Despite the risks, the United States should pursue a forward partnering strategy in several situations: where there is a threat to the United States but substantial local government capacity, or a growing threat to the United States but limited local capacity (and no allied power willing to become involved). In the first case, direct U.S. engagement may not be necessary since the local government has the capacity and political will to target Salafi-jihadist groups with its own forces, undermine terrorist support, combat their narrative, and undercut their finances. One example is Saudi Arabia. Shortly after al Qa'ida lost its sanctuary in Afghanistan, Osama bin Laden began planning to overthrow the Saudi regime and target U.S. personnel in the country. Al Qa'ida's violent campaign began in earnest in early 2003 with an operational core of some 50 people and a wider network of between 300 and 700 people who were prepared to take up arms.[17] Around 2004, Saudi security services captured an al Qa'ida document titled "The Plot," which outlined a strategy to divide al Qa'ida's command structure into five geographic sectors that would oversee infiltration, training, resources, and attacks in its area. The goal, the document noted, was to destabilize the Kingdom, overthrow the government, and establish an Islamic emirate.[18] Gun battles soon erupted between Saudi security forces and al Qa'ida operatives in Jeddah, Khobar, Medda, and other cities. One of al Qa'ida's first major attacks was in Riyadh in May 2003, in which three bombers using RDX-based explosives struck compounds housing Western expatriates, killing 35 people and wounding hundreds. In countering al Qa'ida, the United States provided military, intelligence, financial, and diplomatic assistance to the Saudi government. But the United States did not become directly involved in the campaign.

In the second case, Salafi-jihadist groups may not pose a significant threat to the United States in the near future, but the weakness of the local government makes it desirable to prevent the terrorist threat from worsening. One example is Somalia, where al Shabaab has not plotted attacks against the U.S. homeland, though it has conducted attacks in neighboring countries and includes operatives like Abdikadir Mohammad (or "Ikrima") who have plotted attacks against U.S. targets. Somalia has one of the weakest governments in the world, ranking as the worst-performing government in five of six categories in the World Bank's governance indicators.[19] In addition, foreign militaries participating in the African Union Mission in Somalia could use help from the West, such as additional equipment and financial support, to conduct offensive operations in al Shabaab's strongholds in southern Somalia.

In short, a forward partnering strategy allows the United States to bolster the capacity of local governments by providing security, financial, political, and other aid, but it stops short of direct engagement in a local war.

Strategy 3: Offshore Balancing

The third strategy is offshore balancing.[20] It involves relying on allies and local governments to counter terrorist groups, while avoiding direct engagement or forward partnering. Offshore balancing relies on offshore air, naval, and rapidly deployable ground forces rather than onshore combat power. It might resemble America's military commitment to the Persian Gulf from the end of World War II to before the first Iraq War in 1990–91, when the United States pursued its interests in the region without stationing tanks or fighter aircraft units.[21] This strategy seeks to minimize foreign entanglements. In the Persian Gulf today, for instance, an offshore balancing strategy might involve relying on local allies to counter Salafi-jihadist groups in some countries, but deploying naval vessels—such as a carrier battle group—to the Persian Gulf and utilizing sea-based standoff weapons if there was an imminent threat to the United States. As Harvard professor Stephen Walt argues, "By setting clear priorities and emphasizing reliance on regional allies, it reduces the danger of being drawn into unnecessary conflicts and encourages other states to do more to help us."[22] To be clear, offshore balancing is not an isolationist strategy, since it relies on over-the-horizon air, naval, and ground forces.

Offshore balancing has several benefits. It reduces U.S. financial and blood costs by shifting them to the local government and U.S. allies. It is also less likely than other strategies to inflame local populations that can be coopted by terrorist groups, especially in Muslim countries. Some proponents of offshore balancing point to the period during and after the first Iraq War, when America's decision to leave heavy combat forces on the Arabian Peninsula became the chief rallying cry for Osama bin Laden against the United States and its allies.[23]

But offshore balancing also has several costs. First, it may be too risky in cases where terrorist groups are actively plotting attacks against the United States. Without a U.S. presence, offshore balancing significantly reduces America's ability to influence the situation because allies may not always share U.S. interests. This may be acceptable in cases where terrorist groups are not plotting attacks against the U.S. homeland or its interests overseas. But it is precarious in situations where there is an imminent threat. Second, offshore balancing would not necessarily undermine the Salafi-jihadist narrative. Numerous Salafi jihadists oppose the United States on ideological grounds. The United States is inexorably evil, according to Ayman al-Zawahiri, because of its unwillingness to accept the preeminence of Islamic law.

A Strategic Framework

This framework, supplemented with data from Figure 4.1, suggests that the United States should prioritize its U.S. counterterrorism resources—such as military, intelligence, diplomatic, financial, and law enforcement assistance—more systematically than it has done. It highlights the need for a long-term engagement strategy in Pakistan, Afghanistan, Yemen, and possibly Syria, where there are significant terrorism threats to the United States. Over the long run, the United States needs to devote sufficient resources—from signals collection capabilities to human intelligence collectors—to understand and counter Salafi-jihadist threats in these areas.

In addition, the United States needs a long-term forward partnering relationship with a limited set of countries in Africa (Nigeria, Algeria, Somalia, and Egypt) and the Middle East (Lebanon and Iraq). Building partnership capacity in these countries is equally, if not more, important than with America's Asia-Pacific allies. The Quadrennial Defense Review concludes: "The centerpiece of the Department of Defense commitment to the U.S. Government's rebalance to the Asia-Pacific region continues to be our efforts to modernize and enhance our security alliances with Australia, Japan, the [Republic of Korea], the Philippines, and Thailand."[24] While a security relationship with these Asian countries is important, a failure to substantially improve the capacity of countries in Africa and the Middle East struggling against Salafi-jihadist groups that threaten the United States would unwisely jeopardize America's security. A long-term, sustained forward partnering strategy would also have a more lasting impact than one focused on drone strikes. After all, there is mixed evidence, at best, that drone strikes and broader decapitation strategies alone are effective in defeating terrorist groups.[25] A group can survive a strike when it establishes—or shifts to—a more decentralized leadership structure, possesses an ideology that still has followers, or is able to appoint competent replacements for leaders that have been captured or killed. In addition, successful counterterrorism and counterinsurgency campaigns generally require the local government or its allies to control territory.

Finally, there are several countries—such as Tunisia, Morocco, and Mali—where the United States should encourage allies (including NATO countries) to work with local governments. These steps should not be static, and the United States would need to reassess its options when there are changes in the threat environment or the counterterrorism capacity and willingness of local governments. In addition, regional allies—such as Jordan, Turkey, and Israel—are important for all of these alternatives.

This framework also highlights several U.S. foreign policy issues. First, a complete U.S. withdrawal from Afghanistan by 2016 could seriously jeopardize U.S. security interests because of the continuing presence of Salafi-jihadist and other terrorist groups in Afghanistan and Pakistan. U.S. forces would have little or no mandate and limited or no capabilities to assist the Afghan government if the Taliban threatened to overrun a major city or even topple the government. It would also increase the probability that Afghanistan would be used as a beachhead for al Qa'ida and other militant groups.[26] Of particular concern would be the decision by al Qa'ida leaders in Afghanistan, led by Faruq al-Qatari and Bilal al-'Utaybi, to train operatives involved in attacks in the West. Iraq after the U.S. withdrawal is illustrative: al Qa'ida in Iraq regrouped. It conducted attacks at a high tempo and was instrumental in establishing an affiliate, Jabhat al-Nusrah, in Syria.

A growing civil war or successful Taliban-led insurgency would likely allow al Qa'ida and other terrorist groups, such as Tehreek-e-Taliban Pakistan, the Haqqani network, and Lashkar-e-Taiba, to increase their presence in Afghanistan. Most of these groups expanded their presence in Afghanistan over the past several years and conducted attacks against the U.S. homeland (al Qa'ida and Tehreek-e-Taliban

Pakistan), U.S. forces and U.S. government installations in Afghanistan (Taliban and Haqqani network), or U.S. citizens in the region (Lashkar-e-Taiba and al Qa'ida). In addition, a U.S. military exit from Afghanistan—if it were to happen—could foster a perception among some countries and organizations, however misplaced, that the United States is not a reliable ally. Al Qa'ida and associated movements would likely view a withdrawal of U.S. military forces from Afghanistan as their most important victory since the departure of Soviet forces from Afghanistan in 1989.

Second, the United States should consider a more aggressive strategy to target Salafi-jihadist groups in Syria, either clandestinely or with regional and local allies. According to our data, Salafi jihadists in Syria made up roughly half the total number of Salafi jihadists worldwide in 2013, where they were engaged in a growing number of attacks. In addition, Jabhat al-Nusrah and the Islamic State of Iraq and al-Sham, which were active in Syria, orchestrated approximately two-thirds of al Qa'ida's attacks in 2013. U.S. counterterror operations in Syria are complicated by the fact that the Assad government is an enemy, not an ally. Even if U.S. policymakers choose not to work with the Assad government, U.S. intelligence and special operations units still have several options: directly target Salafi-jihadist groups in Syria through clandestine operations; work through allies such as Jordan, Turkey, or Saudi Arabia; and work through surrogate partners, such as Syrian rebel groups that oppose Jabhat al-Nusrah, the Islamic State of Iraq and al-Sham, and other Salafi jihadists.

The failure to weaken Salafi-jihadist groups in Syria will likely have serious repercussions for the United States, in part because of Syria's proximity to allies like Jordan, Turkey, Israel, and European Union countries. At the moment, Jabhat al-Nusrah and the Islamic State of Iraq and al-Sham appear to be most interested in overthrowing the Assad regime. But it is conceivable that leaders from Jabhat al-Nusrah, the Islamic State of Iraq and al-Sham, or splinter groups could conduct attacks in the region or the West. Their access to foreign fighters, terrorist networks in Europe, and bomb-making expertise suggest that they may already have the capability to plan, support, and orchestrate attacks against the West.

Moreover, as the data in this study suggest, the threat from Salafi-jihadist groups will persist. As a poem entitled "Mujahid's Wish" in the Spring 2013 issue of al Qa'ida's *Inspire* magazine highlighted, the U.S. remains a bitter enemy:

I wish I am in America. It seems odd, right?
Hijra is not the end of a mujahid's ambition.
Walking with an AK is not the end of the road. I used
To think the same as you, until I met brothers in the
Training camps, brothers who look into the enemies'
Barrels and see Jannah. Surprisingly, many of them
Wish to live in America. They have one gentle project
To carry out; detonating even one bomb in any crowded
area. They wish to be lone mujahideen like Tamerlan.
Many of the brothers who made Hijrah from the West
Wish they have a return ticket, returning home
Heading for mom's kitchen. Not to serve the kuffar
With delicious and exotic meals, but to terrorize the
American society until they cease to fight and assault
Muslims.

Brother residing in the West, grab you chance and
Walk steadfastly towards your goal.
As for me here in Yemen, whenever I move around with
Explosives around my waist, I wish I am in America.[27]

APPENDIX

List of Salafi-Jihadist Groups

Table A.1
List of Salafi-Jihadist Groups

Name of Group	Base of Operations	Years
Abdullah Azzam Brigades (Yusuf al-Uyayri Battalions)	Saudi Arabia	2009–present
Abdullah Azzam Brigades (Ziyad al-Jarrah Battalions)	Lebanon	2009–present
Abu Sayyaf Group (ASG)	Philippines	1991–present
Aden Abyan Islamic Army (AAIA)	Yemen	1994–present
Al Ittihad Al Islamiya (AIAI)	Somalia, Ethiopia	1994–2002
Al Qa'ida (core)	Pakistan	1988–present
Al Qa'ida in Aceh (aka Tanzim al Qa'ida Indonesia for Serambi Makkah)	Indonesia	2009–2011
Al Qa'ida in the Arabian Peninsula (Saudi Arabia)	Saudi Arabia	2002–2008
Al Qa'ida in the Arabian Peninsula (Yemen)	Yemen	2008–present
Al Qa'ida in the Islamic Maghreb (AQIM, formerly Salafist Group for Preaching and Combat, GSPC)	Algeria	1998–present
Al Takfir wal al-Hijrah	Israel (Gaza), Egypt (Sinai)	2011–present
Al-Mulathamun (Mokhtar Belmokhtar)	Mali, Libya, Algeria	2012–2013
Al-Murabitun (Mokhtar Belmokhtar)	Mali, Libya, Algeria	2013–present
Alliance for Re-liberation of Somalia-Union of Islamic Courts (ARS/UIC)	Somalia, Eritrea	2006–2009

Table A.1—Continued

Name of Group	Base of Operations	Years
Ansar al-Islam	Iraq	2001–present
Ansar al-Sharia Egypt	Egypt	2012–present
Ansar al-Sharia Libya	Libya	2012–present
Ansar al-Sharia Mali	Mali	2012–present
Ansar al-Sharia Tunisia	Tunisia	2011–present
Ansar Bayt al-Maqdis (aka Ansar Jerusalem)	Israel (Gaza)	2012–present
Ansaru	Nigeria	2012–present
Asbat al-Ansar (AAA)	Lebanon	1985–present
Bangsamoro Islamic Freedom Fighters (BIFF, aka BIFM)	Philippines	2010–present
Boko Haram	Nigeria	2003–present
Chechen Republic of Ichkeria (Basayev faction)	Russia (Chechnya)	1994–2007
East Turkestan Islamic Movement (ETIM, aka Turkestan Islamic Party)	China (Xinjang)	1989–present
Egyptian Islamic Jihad (EIJ)	Egypt	1978–2001
Harakat Ahrar al-Sham al-Islamiyya	Syria	2012–present
Harakat al-Shabaab al-Mujahideen	Somalia	2002–present
Harakat al-Shuada'a al Islamiyah (aka Islamic Martyr's Movement, IMM)	Libya	1996–2007
Harakat Ansar al-Din	Mali	2011–present
Hizbul al Islam	Somalia	2009–2010
Imarat Kavkaz (IK, or Caucasus Emirate)	Russia (Chechnya)	2007–present
Indian Mujahedeen	India	2005–present
Islamic Jihad Union (aka Islamic Jihad Group)	Uzbekistan	2002–present
Islamic Movement of Uzbekistan (IMU)	Uzbekistan, Kyrgyzstan	1997–present
Islamic State of Iraq and al-Sham (ISIS)	Iraq	2004–present
Jabhat al-Nusrah	Syria	2011–present

Table A.1—Continued

Name of Group	Base of Operations	Years
Jaish ul-Adl	Iran	2013–present
Jaish al-Islam (aka Tawhid and Jihad Brigades)	Israel (Gaza), Egypt (Sinai)	2005–present
Jaish al-Ummah (JaU)	Israel (Gaza)	2007–present
Jamaat Ansar Bayt al-Maqdis	Egypt (Sinai)	2011–present
Jamaat Ansarullah (JA)	Tajikistan	2010–present
Jemaah Ansharut Tauhid (JAT)	Indonesia	2008–present
Jemaah Islamiya (JI)	Indonesia, Malaysia, Philippines, Singapore	1993–present
Jondullah	Pakistan	2003–present
Jund al-Sham	Lebanon, Syria, Israel (Gaza), Qatar, Afghanistan	1999–2008
Khalifa Islamiya Mindanao (KIM)	Phillippines	2013–present
Lashkar-e-Taiba (LeT, aka Mansoorian)	Pakistan (Kashmir)	1990–present
Libyan Islamic Fighting Group (LIFG)	Libya	1990–present
Liwa al-Islam	Syria	2011–present
Liwa al-Tawhid	Syria	2012–present
Moroccan Islamic Combatant Group (GICM)	Morocco, Western Europe	1998–present
Movement for Tawhid and Jihad in West Africa (MUJAO)	Mali	2011–2013
Muhammad Jamal Network (MJN)	Egypt	2011–present
Mujahideen Shura Council	Israel (Gaza), Egypt (Sinai)	2011–present
Salafia Jihadia (As-Sirat al Moustaquim)	Morocco	1995–present
Suqour al-Sham	Syria	2011–present
Tawhid waj Jihad	Iraq	1998–2004
Tunisian Combatant Group (TCG)	Tunisia, Western Europe	2000–2011

About the Author

Seth G. Jones is associate director of the International Security and Defense Policy Center at the RAND Corporation, as well as an adjunct professor at Johns Hopkins University's School for Advanced International Studies (SAIS). He previously served as the representative for the commander, U.S. Special Operations Command, to the Assistant Secretary of Defense for Special Operations. Before that, he served as a plans officer and advisor to the commanding general, U.S. Special Operations Forces, in Afghanistan (Combined Forces Special Operations Component Command–Afghanistan). Dr. Jones specializes in counterinsurgency and counterterrorism, including a focus on Afghanistan, Pakistan, and al Qa'ida. He is the author of *Hunting in the Shadows: The Pursuit of al Qa'ida After 9/11* (W. W. Norton, 2012) and *In the Graveyard of Empires: America's War in Afghanistan* (W. W. Norton, 2009), which won the 2010 Council on Foreign Relations Silver Medal for Best Book of the Year. He is also the author of *The Rise of European Security Cooperation* (Cambridge University Press, 2007). Dr. Jones has published articles in a range of journals, such as *Foreign Affairs, Foreign Policy*, and *International Security*, as well as in such newspapers and magazines as the *New York Times*, *Washington Post*, and *Wall Street Journal*. Among his many RAND publications are *Afghanistan's Local War* (2010), *Counterinsurgency in Pakistan* (2010), *How Terrorist Groups End: Lessons for Countering Al Qa'ida* (2009), and *Counterinsurgency in Afghanistan* (2008). Dr. Jones is also coauthor of RAND's series of reports on nation-building. Dr. Jones received his A.B. from Bowdoin College and his M.A. and Ph.D. from the University of Chicago.

Endnotes

Summary

[1] See, for example, John Mueller and Mark G. Stewart, *Terror, Security, and Money: Balancing the Risks, Benefits, and Costs of Homeland Security*, New York: Oxford University Press, 2011; and John J. Mearsheimer, "America Unhinged," *National Interest*, January/February 2014, pp. 9–30. On the weakness of core al Qa'ida, see James R. Clapper, *Worldwide Threat Assessment of the U.S. Intelligence Community*, Washington, D.C.: Office of the Director of National Intelligence, March 2013.

[2] Marc Sageman, "The Stagnation of Research on Terrorism," *The Chronicle of Higher Education*, April 30, 2013. On the response to Sageman, see John Horgan and Jessica Stern, "Terrorism Research Has Not Stagnated," *The Chronicle of Higher Education*, May 8, 2013.

[3] Mearsheimer, 2014, p. 12.

[4] Brian Michael Jenkins, *Stray Dogs and Virtual Armies: Radicalization and Recruitment to Jihadist Terrorism in the United States Since 9/11*, Santa Monica, Calif.: RAND Corporation, OP-343-RC, 2011. As of March 14, 2014: http://www.rand.org/pubs/occasional_papers/OP343.html

[5] Sageman, "The Stagnation of Research on Terrorism," 2013; Marc Sageman, *Leaderless Jihad: Terror Networks in the Twenty-First Century*, Philadelphia: University of Pennsylvania Press, 2008.

[6] Bruce Hoffman, "Al Qaeda's Uncertain Future," *Studies in Conflict and Terrorism*, Vol. 36, 2013, pp. 635–653; Bruce Riedel, "Al Qaeda Is Back," *The Daily Beast*, July 26, 2013.

[7] Andrew Liepman and Philip Mudd, "Al Qaeda Is Down. Al Qaedism Isn't," *CNN*, January 6, 2014. As of March 14, 2014: http://globalpublicsquare.blogs.cnn.com/2014/01/06/al-qaeda-is-down-al-qaedism-isnt/

Chapter One: Introduction

[1] On terrorist waves, see David C. Rapoport, "The Four Waves of Modern Terrorism," in Audrey Kurth Cronin and James M. Ludes, eds., *Attacking Terrorism: Elements of a Grand Strategy*, Washington, D.C.: Georgetown University Press, 2004, pp. 46–73.

[2] See, for example, bin Laden's fatwa published in the London newspaper *Al-Quds al-'Arabi* in February 1998, which noted that "to kill Americans is a personal duty for all Muslims." The text can be found at: http://www.pbs.org/newshour/updates/military/jan-june98/fatwa_1998.html

[3] On Sayyid Qutb's interpretation of armed jihad as a duty, see Sayyid Qutb, *Ma'alim fi al-Tariq* [*Milestones*], Reprint Edition, New Delhi: Islamic Book Service, 2007.

[4] Gilles Kepel, *Muslim Extremism in Egypt: The Prophet and the Pharaoh*, translated by John Rothschild, Berkeley, Calif.: University of California Press, 1993; Olivier Roy, *Globalized Islam: The Search for a New Ummah*, New York: Columbia University Press, 2004, p. 41.

[5] On the term Salafi jihadists, see, for example, Assaf Moghadam, "Motives for Martyrdom: Al-Qaida, Salafi Jihad, and the Spread of Suicide Attacks," *International Security*, Vol. 33, No. 3, Winter 2008/2009, pp. 46–78; Assaf Moghadam, "The Salafi-Jihad as a Religious Ideology," *CTC Sentinel*, Vol. 1, No. 3, February 2008, pp. 14–16. Also see Alain Grignard, "La littérature politique du GIA, des origines à Djamal Zitoun—Esquisse d'une analyse," in F. Dassetto, ed., *Facettes de l'Islam belge*, Louvain-la-Neuve: Academia-Bruylant, 2001.

[6] Brian M. Jenkins, *Will Terrorists Go Nuclear?* Santa Monica, Calif.: RAND Corporation, P-5541, 1975, p. 5. As of March 17, 2014: http://www.rand.org/pubs/papers/P5541.html

[7] On "Islamism," see, for example, Roy, *Globalized Islam*, 2004, p. 2.

[8] On al Qa'ida's organizational structure, see Bruce Hoffman, *Inside Terrorism*, Revised Edition, New York: Columbia University Press, 2006.

[9] On al Qa'ida and its affiliates, see Daniel L. Byman, *Breaking the Bonds Between Al Qa'ida and Its Affiliate Organizations*, Washington, D.C.: Brookings Institution, 2012.

[10] Alexander L. George and Timothy J. McKeown, "Case Studies and Theories of Organizational Decision Making," in Robert F. Coulam and Richard A. Smith, eds., *Advances in Information Processing in Organizations: A Research Annual, Vol. 2*, Greenwich, Conn.: JAI Press, 1985, p. 35.

[11] On transcription challenges, see Roy, *Globalized Islam*, 2004, p. x.

Chapter Two: A Decentralized Movement

[1] Letter from Abu Mohammed al-Jawlani to Abu Bakr al-Baghdadi, May 2013.

[2] Abu Bakr al-Baghdadi, "And Give Glad Tidings to the Believers," Al-Furqan Media Foundation, April 2013.

[3] Audio statement of Abu Mohammed al-Golani, various jihadist forums, May 2013.

[4] Letter from Ayman al-Zawahiri to Abu Bakr al-Baghdadi and Abu Muhammad al-Jawlani, May 2013.

[5] Ibid.

[6] On Abu Khalid al-Suri's death, see Jabhat al-Nusrah, "Statement of Eulogy for the Killing of Sheikh Abu Khalid al-Suri, May Allah Accept Him," February 23, 2014.

[7] Abu Bakr al-Baghdadi, audio message, June 2013.

[8] Ayman al-Zawahiri, "An Urgent Call to Our People in al-Sham," various jihadist forums, January 2014.

[9] Qaedat al-Jihad Organization–General Command, "Statement Regarding the Relationship of the Group of Qaedat al-Jihad with the Group of the Islamic State in Iraq and al-Sham," various jihadist forums, February 2014.

[10] As used here, an organizational structure refers to the key components of a movement, such as its membership, policies, and command and control arrangements. Jeremy M. Weinstein, *Inside Rebellion: The Politics of Insurgent Violence*, New York: Cambridge University Press, 2007, p. 19; Jacob N. Shapiro, *The Terrorist's Dilemma: Managing Violent Covert Organizations,* Princeton, N.J.: Princeton University Press, 2013, pp. 1–25.

[11] "Al Qa'ida's Goals and Structure," AFGP-2002-000078, CTC Harmony Documents; "Interior Organization," AFGP-2002-000080, CTC Harmony Documents; "Camp Acceptance Requirements," Harmony, AFGP-2002-600849, CTC Harmony Documents.

[12] "Al Qa'ida Bylaws," AFGP-2002-600048, CTC Harmony Documents.

[13] World Islamic Front Statement, "Jihad Against Jews and Crusaders," February 23, 1998. The document was signed by Shaykh Usamah Bin-Muhammad Bin-Ladin; Ayman al-Zawahiri, amir of the Jihad Group in Egypt; Abu-Yasir Rifa'i Ahmad Taha, Egyptian Islamic Group; Shaykh Mir Hamzah, secretary of the Jamiat-ul-Ulema-e-Pakistan; and Fazlur Rahman, amir of the Jihad Movement in Bangladesh.

[14] Joseph Felter et al., *Harmony and Disharmony: Exploiting al-Qa'ida's Organizational Vulnerabilities*, West Point, N.Y.: Combating Terrorism Center, 2006, p. 709.

[15] On al Qa'ida's organizational structure, see, for example, Hoffman, *Inside Terrorism*, 2006, p. 285; and Byman, *Breaking the Bonds Between Al-Qa'ida and Its Affiliate Organizations*, 2012.

[16] See, for example, letter from Ayman al-Zawahiri to Abu Bakr al-Baghdadi and Abu Muhammad al-Jawlani, May 2013.

[17] These dates refer to the year in which the affiliate publicly announced that their emirs had sworn *bay'at* to core al Qa'ida leaders.

[18] See, for example, Abu Maryam, "Why Al-Qaeda?" various jihadist websites, March 2014.

[19] Jenkins, *Stray Dogs and Virtual Armies*, 2011.

[20] U.S. Department of Defense, *Protecting the Force: Lessons from Fort Hood*, Washington, D.C.: U.S. Department of Defense Independent Review Related to Fort Hood, January 2010.

[21] Qutb, *Ma'alim fi al-Tariq*.

[22] *The Qur'an*, 5:50.

[23] See, for example, Ibn Taymiyya, *al-'Ubudiyya fi al-Islam*, Cairo: al-Matba'ah al-Salafiyya, undated. On recent references to Ibn Taymiyya, see, for example, Sheikh Ibrahim Ar-Rubaysh, "Allah Will Restrain the Evil Might of Those Who Disbelieve," *Inspire*, No. 11, Spring 1434 (2013), p. 14; and Ayman al-Zawahiri, "Forty-Six Years Since the Setback," Al-Sahab Media Establishment, August 2013.

[24] On Sayyid Qutb's interpretation of armed jihad as a duty, see Qutb, *Ma'alim fi al-Tariq*.

[25] Ayman al-Zawahiri, "The Path of Doom," Al-Sahab Media Establishment, August 2009.

[26] Ayman al-Zawahiri, "Victorious Ummah, Broken Crusade," Al-Sahab Media Establishment, September 2010.

[27] See, for example, Central Intelligence Agency, *Guide to the Analysis of Insurgency*, Washington, D.C.: Central Intelligence Agency, 2012, p. 1.

[28] Max Abrahms, "Why Terrorism Does Not Work," *International Security*, Vol. 31, No. 2, Fall 2006, pp. 51–56. Other studies also find that terrorist campaigns rarely work: Walter Laqueur, *A History of Terrorism*, 3rd ed., New Brunswick, N.J.: Transaction Publishers, 2001, p. 221; Paul Wilkinson, *Terrorism and the Liberal State*, London: Macmillan, 1986, pp. 59, 100; Rapoport, "The Four Waves of Modern Terrorism," 2004, pp. 54–55; Max Abrahms, "The Political Effectiveness of Terrorism Revisited," *Comparative Political Studies*, Vol. 45, No. 3, February 2012, pp. 366–393; and Audrey Kurth Cronin, *How Terrorism Ends: Understanding the Decline and Demise of Terrorist Campaigns*, Princeton, N.J.: Princeton University Press, 2009, ch. 3. For an alternative assessment, see also Eric D. Gould and Esteban F. Klor, "Does Terrorism Work?" *The Quarterly Journal of Economics*, Vol. 125, No. 4, November 2010, pp. 1459–1510.

[29] Abrahms, "Why Terrorism Does Not Work," 2006, pp. 52–56; Jason Lyall and Isaiah Wilson, "Rage Against the Machines: Explaining Outcomes in Counterinsurgency Wars," *International Organization*, Vol. 63, No. 1, Winter 2009, pp. 67–106; Ben Connable and Martin C. Libicki, *How Insurgencies End*, Santa Monica, Calif.: RAND Corporation, MG-965-MCIA, 2010, p. 163 (as of March 17, 2014: http://www.rand.org/pubs/monographs/MG965.html); Laia Balcells and Stathis N. Kalyvas, "Does Warfare Matter? Severity, Duration, and Outcomes of Civil Wars," Institut Català Internacional per la Pau, ICP Working Paper 2012/5, pp. 24–25.

[30] R. Kim Cragin, "Early History of Al Qa'ida," *The Historical Journal*, Vol. 51, No. 4, 2008, pp. 1047–1067.

[31] On *tawhid*, for example, see Ayman al-Zawahiri, "The Dried Dates Idol of Democracy," Fursan Al Balagh Media, August 2013; Ayman al-Zawahiri, "Victorious Ummah, Broken Crusade," Al-Sahab Media Establishment, September 2010.

[32] Sayyid Qutb, *Fi Zilal al-Qur'an* [*In the Shadow of the Qur'an*], translated by M. A. Salahi and A. A. Shamis, Nairobi, Kenya: The Islamic Foundation, 1999; Qutb, *Ma'alim fi al-Tariq*.

[33] See, for example, Al Qa'ida in the Arabian Peninsula, "Convoy of Martyrs," Vol. 2, al-Malahem Media Foundation, July 2013; Sheikh Adil Al-'Abab, "Gains and Benefits of Ansar al-Sharia Control of Parts of the Wiyalahs of Abyan and Shabwa," Ansar al-Mujahideen, 2012; Abu Musab Abdulwadoud, "Congratulations on the Victory of the Grandsons of Omar al-Mukhtar," October 2011; Abu Omar al-Baghdadi, "The Good Harvest," March 2009.

[34] See, for example, the statements of Ansar al Sharia leaders, who argued: "Our people in Libya, know that the way out of today's reality is by returning to the sharia and empowering it, for the true legitimacy is the sharia of Allah, where there is safety, stability, and glory. Say no to the legitimacy of Western democracy." See Ansar al-Sharia Libya, "Statement About the Current Events in Libya," February 20, 2014.

[35] Ayman al-Zawahiri, "The Dried Dates Idol of Democracy," Fursan Al Balagh Media, August 2013.

[36] Ayman al-Zawahiri, "Truth Has Come and Falsehood Has Perished," Al-Sahab Media Establishment, September 2012; Sheikh Adil Al-'Abab, "Gains and Benefits of Ansar al-Sharia Control of Parts of the Wiyalahs of Abyan and Shabwa," Ansar al-Mujahideen, 2012.

[37] See, for example, "Al-Qaida: Constitutional Charter, Rules and Regulations," AFGP-2002-600175, p. 2; "Interior Organization (of al Qa'ida)," AFGP-2002-000080, CTC Harmony Documents, pp. 2–3.

[38] On the establishment of a caliphate, see, for example, Abu Bakr Naji, *The Management of Savagery: The Most Critical Stage Through Which the Ummah Will Pass*, translated and published by the John M. Olin Institute for Strategic Studies at Harvard University, May 23, 2006.

[39] Ayman al-Zawahiri, "General Guidelines for Jihad," Al-Sahab Media Establishment, 2013.

[40] Nasir al-Wuhayshi, "They Plot and Plan, and God Plans Too," Al-Fajr Media Center, February 2009.

[41] Abu Musab Abdulwadoud, "Gaza: Between the Hammer of Jews and Crusaders and the Anvil of Apostates," various jihadist websites, January 2009; Abu Musab Abdulwadoud, "Call to Our Enraged People in Algeria," January 2011. On al Qa'ida views on the French bans, see Yahya Ibrahim, "The West Should Ban the Niqab Covering Its Real Face," *Inspire*, No. 1, Summer 1431 (2010), pp. 19–20.

[42] "Final Statement of the Conference of Islamic State Scholars in Somalia," December 3, 2011.

[43] Ayman al-Zawahiri, "A Document to Support Islam," Al-Sahab Media Establishment, November 2012.

[44] See, for example, Ayman al-Zawahiri, "A Document to Support Islam," Al-Sahab Media Establishment, November 2012; Ayman al-Zawahiri, "Forty-Six Years Since the Setback,"

Al-Sahab Media Establishment, August 2013; Ayman al-Zawahiri, *Knights Under the Prophet's Banner,* trans. Laura Mansfield, Old Tappan, N.J.: TLG Publications, 2002, p. 201.

[45] A good example of a more expansive notion of an al Qa'ida "global insurgency" can be found in David J. Kilcullen, *Counterinsurgency*, New York: Oxford University Press, 2010, pp. 165–227.

[46] Abu Bakr Al-Qurashi Al-Baghdadi, "Allah Will Not Allow Except that His Light Should Be Perfected," Fursan Al-Balagh Media, July 2012.

[47] "An Interview with Abdelmalek Droukdal," *New York Times*, July 1, 2008.

[48] Nasir al-Wuhayshi, "They Plot and Plan, and God Plans Too," Al-Fajr Media Center, February 2009.

[49] Letter from Abu Mus'ab al-Zarqawi to al Qa'ida leaders, circa January 2004. Released by the Harmony Project, Combating Terrorism Center, West Point, N.Y.

[50] See, for example, Abu Bakr Al-Qurashi Al-Baghdadi, "Allah Will Not Allow Except that His Light Should Be Perfected," Fursan Al-Balagh Media, July 2012.

[51] Abu Mohammed al-Jawlani, "The Coming Days Will Be Better Than Past Ones," Fursan Al-Balagh Media, August 2013.

[52] Ayman al-Zawahiri, "Forty-Six Years Since the Setback," Al-Sahab Media Establishment, August 2013; Ayman al-Zawahiri, "Truth Has Come and Falsehood Has Perished," Al-Sahab Media Establishment, September 2012.

[53] Letter from Zawahiri to Zarqawi, July 9, 2005.

[54] Letter from Nasir al-Wuhayshi to Emir of Al Qa'ida in the Islamic Maghreb, May 21, 2012, Associated Press collection. The document is part of a cache of documents that the Associated Press found on the floor in a building occupied by al Qa'ida fighters in Mali.

[55] Sheikh Adil Al-'Abab, "Gains and Benefits of Ansar al-Sharia Control of Parts of the Wiyalahs of Abyan and Shabwa," Ansar al-Mujahideen, 2012.

[56] On the al Qa'ida in Iraq and the Awakening, see Major Niel Smith and Colonel Sean MacFarland, "Anbar Awakens: The Tipping Point," *Military Review*, March–April 2008, pp. 65–76; Mitchell B. Reiss, *Negotiating with Evil: When to Talk to Terrorists*, New York: Open Road, 2010, pp. 177–220; and Seth G. Jones, *Hunting in the Shadows: The Pursuit of Al Qa'ida Since 9/11*, New York: W. W. Norton, 2012.

[57] Ayman al-Zawahiri, "General Guidelines for Jihad," Al-Sahab Media Establishment, September 2013.

[58] Ayman al-Zawahiri, *Winds of Paradise*, Second Edition, Al-Sahab Media Establishment, March 2014.

[59] Cronin, *How Terrorism Ends,* 2009, pp. 13–34.

[60] Felter, *Harmony and Disharmony*, 2006, p. 9.

[61] "You Are Held Responsible Only for Thyself—Part One," Al-Sahab Media Establishment, June 2011.

[62] Richard Clutterbuck, *Conflict and Violence in Singapore and Malaysia, 1945–1983*, Boulder, Colo.: Westview Press, 1985, pp. 170–171.

[63] Clutterbuck, *Conflict and Violence in Singapore and Malaysia*, 1985, pp. 198–199.

[64] John Howell, "Horn of Africa: Lessons from the Sudan Conflict," *International Affairs*, Vol. 54, No. 3, 1978, p. 425.

[65] On principal-agent problems and insurgency, see Weinstein, *Inside Rebellion*, 2007, p. 130; and Shapiro, *The Terrorist's Dilemma*, 2013, pp. 101–130.

[66] Weinstein, *Inside Rebellion*, 2007, pp. 129–130.

[67] Weinstein, *Inside Rebellion*, pp. 43–44; Abdulkader H. Sinno, *Organizations at War in Afghanistan and Beyond*, Ithaca, N.Y.: Cornell University Press, 2008, p. 70.

[68] On networked strategies, see John Arquilla and David Ronfeldt, *Networks and Netwars: The Future of Terror, Crime, and Militancy*, Santa Monica, Calif.: RAND Corporation, MR-1382-OSD, 2001. As of March 17, 2014: http://www.rand.org/pubs/monograph_reports/MR1382.html

[69] Abu Mus'ab al-Suri, "The Jihadi Experiences: The Schools of Jihad," *Inspire*, No. 1, Summer 1431 (2010), p.49.

[70] Abu Mus'ab al-Suri, "The Jihadi Experiences: The Military Theory of Open Fronts," *Inspire*, No. 4, Winter 1431 (2010), p. 31.

[71] Louis Beam, "Leaderless Resistance," *Seditionist*, No. 12, February 1992, p. 5.

[72] John Arquilla and David Ronfeldt, "The Advent of Netwar," in Arquilla and Ronfeldt, eds., *In Athena's Camp: Preparing for Conflict in the Information Age*, Santa Monica, Calif.: RAND Corporation, MR-880-OSD/RC, 1997. As of March 17, 2014: http://www.rand.org/pubs/monograph_reports/MR880.html

[73] The high, moderate, and low codings come from the Non-State Actor Data Set. See David E. Cunningham, Kristian Skrede Gleditsch, and Idean Salehyan, *Codebook for the Non-State Actor Data*, University of North Texas, Version 3.3, January 2012.

[74] The data are from Seth G. Jones, *The Theory and Conduct of Insurgency*, draft manuscript, December 2013.

[75] Lyall and Wilson, "Rage Against the Machines," 2009, pp. 67–106; Ivan Arreguín-Toft, *How the Weak Win Wars: A Theory of Asymmetric Conflict*, New York: Cambridge University Press, 2005, pp. 23–47.

[76] Qaedat al-Jihad Organization–General Command, "Statement Regarding the Relationship of the Group of Qaedat al-Jihad with the Group of the Islamic State in Iraq and al-Sham," various jihadist forums, February 2014.

Chapter Three: Growing Capabilities

[1] See, for example, U.S. Army, *Case Study: Terrorist Attack on Westgate Mall, Nairobi, Kenya: 21–24 September 2013*, Washington, D.C., 2014; Kevin Yorke, *Analysis of Al-Shabaab's Attack at the Westgate Mall in Nairobi*, Kenya, New York: New York City Police Department, 2013.

[2] "From the Editor," Gaidi Mtaani, Dhul Hijra 1434, toleo 4, p. 1.

[3] For the low estimate, the number of fighters increased by 251 percent from 2010 to 2013. For the high estimate, the number of fighters increased by 121 percent during the same period.

[4] Estimates based on multiple sources, including data from the Global Terrorism Database at the University of Maryland's National Consortium for the Study of Terrorism and Responses to Terrorism (START); Jane's World Insurgency and Terrorism database; and author estimates.

[5] U.S. Department of State, *Terrorist Designations of the Muhammad Jamal Network and Muhammad Jamal*, Washington, D.C.: Office of the Spokesperson, U.S. Department of State, October 2013.

[6] See, for example, Ansar Bayt al-Maqdis, "Fight Them Until There Is No Fitnah," September 2013, video released on multiple jihadist websites; Mujahidin Shura Council, "Response of the Lions to the Aggressions of the Jews: Shelling Zionist Sderot with Three Rockets," September 2012, video released on multiple jihadist web sites.

[7] John O'Neil, "U.S. Renews Libyan Ties After Break of 34 Years," *New York Times*, May 15, 2006.

[8] See, for example, Ansar al-Sharia Libya, Statement About the Current Events in Libya, February 2014.

[9] Ahmed Maher, "Meeting Mohammad Ali al-Zahawi," BBC, September 18, 2012.

[10] The insignia used by the groups, which includes the phrase "Your Sons at Your Service," was posted on the group's Twitter site (https://twitter.com/AnsarShariaa_ly).

[11] On Belmokhtar's views, see, for example, his interview with Mauritanian press, available at: http://occident2.blogspot.com/2011/11/interview-with-mukhtar-bin-muhammad.html (accessed December 19, 2013). Also see his training videos, such as those available at: http://www.youtube.com/watch?v=uTKFB-G-fvE (accessed December 19, 2013).

[12] "Belmokhtar's Militants 'Merge' with Mali's MUJAO," BBC, August 22, 2013.

[13] Lin Noueihed, "Radical Islamists Urge Bigger Role for Islam in Tunisia," Reuters, May 21, 2012.

[14] "Branding 'Ansar al-Sharia' as Terrorist Organisation Based on Establishing Investigations," Agence Tunis Afrique Presse, August 28, 2013.

[15] On Ansar al-Din's ties to al Qa'ida in the Islamic Maghreb, see U.S. Department of State, Terrorist Designations of Ansar al-Dine, Washington, D.C., March 2013.

[16] See, for example, Christopher S. Chivvis and Andrew Liepman, *North Africa's Menace: AQIM's Evolution and the U.S. Policy Response*, Santa Monica, Calif.: RAND Corporation, RR-415-OSD, 2013. As of March 17, 2014: http://www.rand.org/pubs/research_reports/RR415.html

[17] "Nigerian Islamic Uprising Has Harmed 3 Million," *Washington Post*, March 29, 2014.

[18] Youssef al-Qaradawi posted the fatwa on his website: http://www.qaradawi.net/ (accessed December 19, 2013).

[19] Estimates based on multiple sources, including data from the Global Terrorism Database at the University of Maryland's National Consortium for the Study of Terrorism and Responses to Terrorism (START); Jane's World Insurgency and Terrorism database; and author estimates.

[20] Ziad al-Jarrah was the name of a Lebanese hijacker who participated in the September 11, 2001, hijacking and crash of United Flight 93.

[21] See, for example, Peter Bergen and Jennifer Rowland, "Al Qaeda Controls More Territory than Ever in Middle East," CNN, January 7, 2014. As of January 16, 2014: http://www.cnn.com/2014/01/07/opinion/bergen-al-qaeda-terrority-gains/

[22] Author interview with government officials from Europe and the Middle East, Brussels, and Washington, November and December 2013.

[23] Bill Roggio, "Al Nusrah Front Imposes Sharia in Eastern Syrian Town," *Long War Journal*, January 30, 2013.

[24] The data on attacks by other Salafi-jihadist groups were much less reliable, so I have not included the number of attacks by Salafi jihadists outside of al Qa'ida.

[25] We coded an attack as "both" if it included a Western target located in a near-enemy country, in part because the attack generally killed or injured both near- and far-enemy victims.

[26] Al Qa'ida in the Arabian Peninsula's media arm, al-Malahim, released a Twitter statement on @shomokhalislam regarding the December 5, 2013, and other attacks. See also IHS Jane's, Al Qa'ida in the Arabian Peninsula, December 2013, accessed via Jane's World Insurgency and Terrorism database on December 19, 2013; and "Al-Qaeda Claims Responsibility Over DOD Attack," *Yemen Post*, December 7, 2013.

[27] IHS Jane's, Al Shabaab, December 2013, accessed via Jane's World Insurgency and Terrorism database on December 19, 2013.

[28] "President Hassan 'Al-Shabaab Will Never Stop Us Making Huge Progress in Somalia,'" Wacaal Media Network, November 8, 2013; "Deadly Explosion Rocks Mogadishu Hotel," *Al Jazeera*, November 11, 2013.

[29] IHS Jane's, Al Shabaab, December 2013, accessed via Jane's World Insurgency and Terrorism database on December 19, 2013.

[30] Estimate based on multiple sources, including data from the Global Terrorism Database at the University of Maryland's National Consortium for the Study of Terrorism and Responses to Terrorism (START); Jane's World Insurgency and Terrorism database; and author estimates.

[31] Syrian Observatory for Human Rights, Facebook Page, February 2013; Bill Roggio, "Al Nusrah Front Spearheads Capture of Syrian Dam, Claims Suicide Assault," *Long War Journal*, February 11, 2013.

[32] See, for example, Bill Roggio, "'Islamist' Factions Seize Syrian Airbase," *Long War Journal*, February 12, 2013.

[33] Author interview with European government officials, Brussels, November 2013. Also see "€20 Million Ransom Paid to Free French Hostages," *The Local*, October 30, 2013.

[34] United Nations Office for the Coordinator of Humanitarian Affairs, "Northeast Nigeria: 2013 in Review," *Humanitarian Bulletin*, No. 8, December 2013, pp. 1–4.

[35] IHS Jane's, Boko Haram, October 2013, accessed via Jane's World Insurgency and Terrorism database on December 13, 2013.

[36] Dalatou Mamane and Rukmimi Callimachi, "Official: Shooting Breaks Out Near Niger Base," Associated Press, June 11, 2013.

[37] See, for example, Ansar Bayt al-Maqdis, "Fight Them Until There Is No Fitnah," September 2013, video released on multiple jihadist websites.

[38] U.S. Department of State, *Terrorist Designations of the Muhammad Jamal Network and Muhammad Jamal*, Washington, D.C., October 2013.

[39] James R. Clapper, *Worldwide Threat Assessment of the U.S. Intelligence Community*, Washington, D.C.: Office of the Director of National Intelligence, January 2014.

[40] Jenkins, *Stray Dogs and Virtual Armies*, 2011.

[41] On Westgate, see U.S. Army, *Case Study: Terrorist Attack on Westgate Mall, Nairobi, Kenya*, 2014; Yorke, *Analysis of Al-Shabaab's Attack at the Westgate Mall in Nairobi, Kenya*, 2013.

[42] Committee on Homeland Security, *Al Shabaab: Recruitment and Radicalization Within the Muslim American Community and the Threat to the Homeland*, Majority Investigative Report, Washington, D.C.: U.S. House of Representatives, July 27, 2011, p. 2.

[43] See, for example, Jehad Serwad Mostafa, Rewards for Justice, U.S. Department of Justice. As of January 22, 2014: http://www.rewardsforjustice.net/index.cfm?page=mostafa&language=english

[44] Author interview with government officials from Europe and the Middle East, April and May 2013.

[45] Hegghammer, "The Rise of Muslim Foreign Fighters," 2011, pp. 53–94.

[46] Ann Hironaka, *Neverending Wars: The International Community, Weak States, and the Perpetuation of Civil War*, Cambridge, Mass.: Harvard University Press, 2005; James D. Fearon and David Laitin, "Ethnicity, Insurgency, and Civil War," *American Political Science Review*, Vol. 97, No. 1, February 2003, pp. 75–90. On the importance of building institutions, see Roland Paris, *At War's End: Building Peace After Civil Conflict*, New York: Cambridge University Press, 2004.

[47] World Bank, *Governance Matters 2006: Worldwide Governance Indicators*, Washington, D.C., 2006, p. 2.

[48] Max Weber, "Politics as a Vocation," in H. H. Gerth and C. Wright Mills, eds., *From Max Weber: Essays in Sociology*, New York: Oxford University Press, 1958, p. 78.

[49] World Bank, *Reforming Public Institutions and Strengthening Governance*, Washington, D.C., 2000; Jessica Einhorn, "The World Bank's Mission Creep," *Foreign Affairs*, Vol. 80, No. 5, 2001, pp. 22–35.

[50] Hironaka, *Neverending Wars*, 2005, pp. 42–46.

[51] Stathis N. Kalyvas, *The Logic of Violence in Civil War*, New York: Cambridge University Press, 2006, p. 216; Timothy P. Wickham-Crowley, *Guerrillas and Revolution in Latin America: A Comparative Study of Insurgents and Regimes Since 1956*, Princeton, N.J.: Princeton University Press, 1992, p. 35.

[52] Jane Stromseth, David Wippman, and Rosa Brooks, *Can Might Make Rights? Building the Rule of Law After Military Interventions*, New York: Cambridge University Press, 2006, pp. 137–140.

[53] Daniel L. Byman, "Friends Like These: Counterinsurgency and the War on Terrorism," *International Security*, Vol. 31, No. 2, Fall 2006, pp. 79–115; Daniel L. Byman, *Going to War with the Allies You Have: Allies, Counterinsurgency, and the War on Terrorism*, Carlisle, Pa.: U.S. Army War College, November 2005.

[54] Fearon and Laitin, "Ethnicity, Insurgency, and Civil War," 2003, pp. 75–76.

[55] Michael W. Doyle and Nicholas Sambanis, *Making War and Building Peace*, Princeton, N.J.: Princeton University Press, 2006, p. 5.

[56] Hironaka, *Neverending Wars*, 2005, p. 45.

[57] World Bank, Worldwide Governance Indicators Data Set, accessed December 16, 2013.

[58] Ibid.

[59] Thomas Hegghammer, "The Recruiter's Dilemma: Signaling and Rebel Recruitment Tactics," *Journal of Peace Research*, Vol. 50, No. 1, 2012, pp. 3–16; Max Abrahms, "What Terrorists Really Want: Terrorist Motives and Counterterrorism Strategy," *International Security*, Vol. 32, No. 4, Spring 2008, pp. 100–101.

[60] On identity and strategic culture, see, for example, Alexander Wendt, *Social Theory of International Politics*, New York: Cambridge University Press, 1999; Peter J. Katzenstein, *The Culture of National Security: Norms and Identity in World Politics*, New York: Columbia University Press, 1996.

[61] See, for example, Umar Farouk Abdulmutallab Comments, Training Video of Abdulmutallab, Al Malahim Media Foundation (al Qa'ida in the Arabian Peninsula), released in 2010.

[62] Rohan Gunaratna, "The Terrorist Training Camps of al Qaida," in James J. F. Forest, ed., *The Making of a Terrorist: Recruitment, Training and Root Causes*, Westport, Conn.: Praeger, 2006, pp. 172–193.

[63] See, for example, the study of Sayyid Imam Abd al-Aziz al-Sharif's works in al Qa'ida camps. Muhammad Hasan Khalil al-Hakim, "Jihad Revisions: Truths and Presuppositions," June 11, 2007, posted on a jihadist website.

[64] Omar Nasiri, *Inside the Jihad: My Life with Al Qaeda*, Cambridge, Mass.: Perseus, 2006. Also see the experiences of al Qa'ida operatives José Padilla and Najibullah Zazi. Declaration of Mr. Jeffrey N. Rapp, Director, Joint Intelligence Task Force for Combating Terrorism, submitted for the Court's consideration in the matter of *José Padilla v. Commander C. T. Hanft, USN, Commander, Consolidated Naval Brig*, Case Number 04-CV-2221-26AJ; *United States of America v. Najibullah Zazi*, United States District Court, Eastern District of New York, Docket No.: 09 CR 663 (S-1), Transcript of Criminal Cause for Pleading, February 22, 2010.

[65] Hegghammer, "The Recruiter's Dilemma," 2012; Omar Nasiri, *Inside the Jihad*, 2006.

[66] On the transnational movement of terrorists, see, for example, Thomas Hegghammer, "Should I Stay or Should I Go? Explaining Variation in Western Jihadists' Choice Between Domestic and Foreign Fighting," *American Political Science Review*, Vol. 107, No. 1, February 2013, pp. 1–15; Thomas Hegghammer, "The Rise of Muslim Foreign Fighters: Islam and the Globalization of Jihad," *International Security*, Vol. 35, No. 3, 2011, pp. 53–94.

[67] United Nations, *Security Council Al-Qaida Sanctions Committee Adds Two Entries to Its Sanctions List*, New York, October 2013.

[68] The data reflect those who said they are "very favorable or "somewhat favorable" to al Qa'ida. Note that the number of those very or somewhat favorable to al Qa'ida rose in Turkey and Palestinian territory. Pew Research Center, *Muslim Publics Share Concerns About Extremist Groups: Much Diminished Support for Suicide Bombing*, Washington, D.C.: Global Attitudes Project, September 2013, p. 19.

[69] Ibid., p. 1.

Chapter Four: Strategic Options

[1] U.S. Department of Defense, *Quadrennial Defense Review 2014*, Washington, D.C., 2014, pp. IV, 4.

[2] On counterterrorism strategy, see Martha Crenshaw, "Terrorism, Strategies, and Grand Strategies," in Audrey Kurth Cronin and James M. Ludes, eds., *Attacking Terrorism: Elements of a Grand Strategy*, Washington, D.C.: Georgetown University Press, 2004, pp. 74–93; Her Majesty's Government, *CONTEST: The United Kingdom's Strategy for Countering Terrorism*, Cm 8123, London: The Stationery Office, July 2011; and The White House, *National Strategy for Counterterrorism*, Washington, D.C., June 2011.

[3] On strategy, see John J. Mearsheimer, *Conventional Deterrence*, Ithaca, N.Y.: Cornell University Press, 1983, pp. 2, 28–29. For counterterrorism and counterterrorism strategies, see Arreguín-Toft, *How the Weak Win Wars*, 2005; Jerry M. Tinker, ed., *Strategies of Revolutionary Warfare*, New Delhi: S. Chand & Co., 1969; Gérard Chaliand, *Guerrilla Strategies:*

An Historical Anthology from the Long March to Afghanistan, Berkeley, Calif.: University of California Press, 1982; and B. H. Liddell Hart, *Strategy: The Indirect Approach*, New Delhi: Pentagon Press, 2012, p. 335.

[4] This use of strategy is different than the concept of "grand strategy," which is the broader process by a government to determine vital security interests, identify the threats to those interests, and decide how best to employ political, military, economic, and other resources to protect those interests. On grand strategy, see Barry R. Posen, *Restraint: A New Foundation for U.S. Grand Strategy*, Ithaca, N.Y.: Cornell University Press, forthcoming; Michael E. Brown, Owen R. Coté, Sean M. Lynn-Jones, and Steven Miller, eds., *America's Strategic Choices*, Cambridge, Mass.: MIT Press, 2000; Stephen M. Walt, "More or Less: The Debate on U.S. Grand Strategy," *Foreign Policy*, January 3, 2013; Stephen G. Brooks, G. John Eikenberry, and William C. Wohlforth, "Lean Forward: In Defense of American Engagement," *Foreign Affairs*, Vol. 92, No. 1, January/February 2013, pp. 130–142.

[5] Countries were coded according to the following qualitative criteria for groups operating there. Score of 3.0: Group engaged in active plotting of attacks against the U.S. homeland and U.S. target overseas (such as embassies); Score of 2.5: Group engaged in limited plotting against the U.S. homeland, but active plotting against U.S. targets overseas; Score of 2.0: Group not engaged in plotting against the U.S. homeland, but active plotting against U.S. targets overseas; Score of 1.5: Group not engaged in plotting against the U.S. homeland, but limited plotting against U.S. targets overseas; Score of 1.0: No groups involved in serious plots against the U.S. homeland or U.S. targets overseas.

[6] The focus of this chapter is on how to deal with Salafi-jihadist groups that are primarily located overseas, not on U.S. soil.

[7] Byman, "Friends Like These," 2006, pp. 79–115.

[8] For an overview of primacy, see Stephen M. Walt, *Taming American Power: The Global Response to U.S. Primacy*, New York: W. W. Norton, 2005, pp. 29–61; Barry R. Posen and Andrew L. Ross, "Competing Visions for U.S. Grand Strategy," *International Security*, Vol. 21, No. 3, Winter 1996–1997, pp. 5–53.

[9] See, for example, Barry R. Posen, "Pull Back: The Case for a Less Activist Foreign Policy," *Foreign Affairs*, Vol. 92, No. 1, January/February 2013, pp. 116–128.

[10] Depending on a Salafi-jihadist group's organizational structure, capabilities, support base, and other factors, an engagement strategy might involve decapitation (catching or killing the group's leadership), negotiations, or other options. On how terrorist groups end, see, for example, Cronin, *How Terrorism Ends*, 2009; Seth G. Jones and Martin C. Libicki, *How Terrorist Groups End: Lessons for Countering al Qa'ida*, Santa Monica, Calif.: RAND Corporation, MG-741-1-RC, 2008. As of March 18, 2014: http://www.rand.org/pubs/monographs/MG741-1.html

[11] As outlined in the National Security Act of 1947, covert action refers to "an activity or activities of the United States Government to influence political, economic, or military conditions abroad, where it is intended that the role of the United States Government will not be apparent or acknowledged publicly." See National Security Act of 1947, Section 503e. In addition, Title 50 of the U.S. Code allows the U.S. military to conduct covert action under

a CIA-run operation. See United States Code, Title 50: War and National Defense, Section 413.

[12] Posen, "Pull Back," 2013, pp. 116–128.

[13] Jones, *Hunting in the Shadows*, 2012.

[14] On forward partnering and U.S. grand strategy, see Frank G. Hoffman, "Forward Partnership: A Sustainable American Strategy," *Orbis*, Vol. 57, No. 1, Winter 2013, pp. 20–40; and Hans Binnendijk, "Rethinking U.S. Security Strategy," *New York Times*, March 24, 2013.

[15] Al Shabaab, "The Experience of Our Brothers in Somalia," undated.

[16] Ibid., p. 6.

[17] Thomas Hegghammer, *Jihad in Saudi Arabia: Violence and Pan-Islamism Since 1979*, New York: Cambridge University Press, 2010, p. 181. On al Qa'ida estimates, also see Nawaf Obaid and Anthony Cordesman, *Al-Qaeda in Saudi Arabia: Asymmetric Threats and Islamic Extremists*, Washington, D.C.: Center for Strategic and International Studies, 2005, p. 20.

[18] Hegghammer, *Jihad in Saudi Arabia*, 2010; Bruce Riedel and Bilal Y. Saab, "Al Qaeda's Third Front: Saudi Arabia," *Washington Quarterly*, Vol. 31, No. 2, Spring 2008, pp. 33–46.

[19] The data are for 2012. World Bank, Worldwide Governance Indicators Data Set, accessed January 8, 2014.

[20] On offshore balancing and U.S. grand strategy, see Christopher Layne, "From Preponderance to Offshore Balancing," *International Security*, Vol. 22, No. 1, Summer 1997, pp. 112–124; Christopher Layne, *The Peace of Illusions: American Grand Strategy from 1940 to the Present*, Ithaca, N.Y.: Cornell University Press, 2006; John J. Mearsheimer, "Imperial by Design," *The National Interest*, January/February 2011, pp. 31–34; Mearsheimer, *The Tragedy of Great Power Politics*, New York: W. W. Norton, 2001, pp. 257–259; and Robert Pape and James Feldman, *Cutting the Fuse: The Explosion of Global Suicide Terrorism and How to Stop It*, Chicago: University of Chicago Press, 2010, pp. 12–13, 333–335.

[21] Pape and Feldman, *Cutting the Fuse*, 2010, p. 12.

[22] Walt, *Taming American Power*, 2005, p. 223.

[23] Pape and Feldman, *Cutting the Fuse*, 2010, p. 12.

[24] U.S. Department of Defense, *Quadrennial Defense Review 2014*, p. 16.

[25] Cronin, *How Terrorism Ends*, 2009; Jenna Jordan, "When Heads Roll: Assessing the Effectiveness of Leadership Decapitation," *Security Studies*, Vol. 18, No. 4, December 2009, pp. 719–755; Stephen T. Hosmer, *Operations Against Enemy Leaders*, Santa Monica, Calif.: RAND Corporation, MR-1385-AF, 2001. As of March 20, 2014: http://www.rand.org/pubs/monograph_reports/MR1385.html On the effectiveness of drones, see Patrick B. Johnston, "Does Decapitation Work? Assessing the Effectiveness of Leadership Targeting in Counterinsurgency Campaigns," *International Security*, Vol. 36, No. 4, Spring 2012, pp. 47–49.

[26] Robert D. Blackwill, "Plan B in Afghanistan," *Foreign Affairs*, Vol. 90, No. 1, January/February 2011, pp. 42–50.

[27] Sheikh Ibrahim Ar-Rubaysh, "Allah Will Restrain the Evil Might of Those Who Disbelieve," *Inspire*, No. 11, Spring 1434 (2013), pp. 36–37.

Index